Managing Tourette Syndrome

MW00669406

EDITOR-IN-CHIEF

David H. Barlow, Ph.D.

SCIENTIFIC
ADVISORY BOARD

Anne Marie Albano, Ph.D.

Gillian Butler, Ph.D.

David M. Clark, Ph.D.

Edna B. Foa, Ph.D.

Paul J. Frick, Ph.D.

Jack M. Gorman, M.D.

Kirk Heilbrun, Ph.D.

Robert J. McMahon, Ph.D.

Peter E. Nathan, Ph.D.

Christine Maguth Nezu, Ph.D.

Matthew K. Nock, Ph.D.

Paul Salkovskis, Ph.D.

Bonnie Spring, Ph.D.

Gail Steketee, Ph.D.

John R. Weisz, Ph.D.

G. Terence Wilson, Ph.D.

Managing Tourette Syndrome

A BEHAVIORAL INTERVENTION FOR CHILDREN AND ADULTS

Therapist Guide

Douglas W. Woods • John C. Piacentini
Susanna W. Chang • Thilo Deckersbach
Golda S. Ginsburg • Alan L. Peterson
Lawrence D. Scahill • John T. Walkup
Sabine Wilhelm

OXFORD
UNIVERSITY PRESS

2008

OXFORD

UNIVERSITY PRESS

Oxford University Press, Inc., publishes works that further
Oxford University's objective of excellence
in research, scholarship, and education.

Oxford   New York
Auckland   Cape Town   Dar es Salaam   Hong Kong   Karachi
Kuala Lumpur   Madrid   Melbourne   Mexico City   Nairobi
New Delhi   Shanghai   Taipei   Toronto

With offices in
Argentina   Austria   Brazil   Chile   Czech Republic   France   Greece
Guatemala   Hungary   Italy   Japan   Poland   Portugal   Singapore
South Korea   Switzerland   Thailand   Turkey   Ukraine   Vietnam

Copyright © 2008 by Oxford University Press, Inc.

Published by Oxford University Press, Inc.
198 Madison Avenue, New York, New York 10016

www.oup.com

Oxford is a registered trademark of Oxford University Press

All rights reserved. No part of this publication may be reproduced,
stored in a retrieval system, or transmitted, in any form or by any means,
electronic, mechanical, photocopying, recording, or otherwise,
without the prior permission of Oxford University Press.

CIP data on file
ISBN 978-0-19-534128-7

18 17 16 15 14

Printed in the United States of America
on acid-free paper

About Treatments*ThatWork*™

Stunning developments in healthcare have taken place over the last several years, but many of our widely accepted interventions and strategies in mental health and behavioral medicine have been brought into question by research evidence as not only lacking benefit, but perhaps, inducing harm. Other strategies have been proven effective using the best current standards of evidence, resulting in broad-based recommendations to make these practices more available to the public. Several recent developments are behind this revolution. First, we have arrived at a much deeper understanding of pathology, both psychological and physical, which has led to the development of new, more precisely targeted interventions. Second, our research methodologies have improved substantially, such that we have reduced threats to internal and external validity, making the outcomes more directly applicable to clinical situations. Third, governments around the world and healthcare systems and policymakers have decided that the quality of care should improve, that it should be evidence based, and that it is in the public's interest to ensure that this happens (Barlow, 2004; Institute of Medicine, 2001).

Of course, the major stumbling block for clinicians everywhere is the accessibility of newly developed evidence-based psychological interventions. Workshops and books can go only so far in acquainting responsible and conscientious practitioners with the latest behavioral healthcare practices and their applicability to individual patients. This new series, Treatments*ThatWork*™, is devoted to communicating these exciting new interventions to clinicians on the frontlines of practice.

The manuals and workbooks in this series contain step-by-step detailed procedures for assessing and treating specific problems and diagnoses. But this series also goes beyond the books and manuals by providing ancillary materials that will approximate the supervisory process in assisting practitioners in the implementation of these procedures in their practice.

In our emerging healthcare system, the growing consensus is that evidence-based practice offers the most responsible course of action for the mental health professional. All behavioral healthcare clinicians deeply desire to provide the best possible care for their patients. In this series, our aim is to close the dissemination and information gap and make that possible.

This therapist guide addresses the treatment of Tourette syndrome (TS) in children and adults (ages 9 and older). The goal of this 11-session program is to teach the patient effective tic management skills rather than to cure the tic disorder. A useful adjunct or alternative to medication, the treatment described in this guide is scientifically based and proven effective. Over the course of the program, individuals are taught how to be aware of their tics, how to substitute other behaviors for their tics, and how to avoid factors that may make their tics worse. Relaxation techniques to reduce stress, which can exacerbate tic symptoms, are also a part of therapy. Relapse prevention strategies help patients keep up their progress after treatment has ended.

Complete with step-by-step instructions for running sessions, as well as lists of materials needed, session outlines, and copies of forms necessary for treatment, this therapist guide provides you with all the information you need to successfully treat tic disorders. Also available is a corresponding workbook for parents and their children, as well as a workbook designed specifically for your adolescent and adult clients. Together, these books form a complete treatment package that clinicians will find to be a welcome addition to their armamentarium.

David H. Barlow, Editor-in-Chief,
Treatments *ThatWork*™
Boston, MA

References

Barlow, D. H. (2004). Psychological treatments. *American Psychologist, 59*, 869–878.

Institute of Medicine. (2001). *Crossing the quality chasm: A new health system for the 21st century*. Washington, DC: National Academy Press.

Contents

Chapter 1 | *Introductory Information for Therapists*

Background Information and Purpose of This Program

Treatment for those with tic disorders, including Tourette syndrome (TS; also referred to as Tourette's disorder), has primarily been conducted by psychiatrists and neurologists. Medications have been the treatment of choice and can be effective in managing symptoms. However, a useful adjunct or alternative to medication has emerged. Behavior therapy for tic disorders has been discussed in the literature for more than 30 years, although many mental health providers remain unfamiliar with this treatment (Marcks, Woods, Teng, & Twohig, 2004).

This manual was written to familiarize therapists with this therapeutic approach. The treatment is an 11-session package for children and adults (ages 9 and older). Psychoeducation about tic disorders is blended with multiple components of behavior therapy, including habit reversal training (HRT), relaxation training, and function-based treatments. It is important to understand that the goal of this program is to teach the patient effective tic management skills rather than to cure the tic disorder.

Given the higher prevalence of tic disorders in pediatric populations compared to adults, this therapist guide focuses on the treatment of children. Nevertheless, modifications that may be useful for adults are offered throughout (see "Working With Adults" sections in session chapters), and separate adult-focused and parent (i.e, child-focused) workbooks are available. Although the term "TS" is used throughout the manual, the treatment can be applied to the other tic disorder diagnoses, including chronic motor or vocal tic disorder and transient tic disorder (TTD).

Tic Disorders

Clinical Characteristics of TS

TS is a chronic, neurobehavioral disorder of childhood onset characterized by motor and vocal tics. Table 1.1 provides examples of various simple and complex, motor and vocal tics. TS symptoms often appear between the ages of 5 and 7 years and typically begin with eye blinking and facial movements. Motor tics often precede the onset of vocal tics and simple tics often precede the onset of complex tics (Leckman, King, & Cohen, 1999).

Table 1.1 List of Simple and Complex Tics

Simple motor tics	Complex motor tics
Eye blinking	Eye movements
Eye movements	Mouth movements
Nose movements	Facial movements or expressions
Mouth movements	Head gestures or movements
Facial grimace	Shoulder movements
Head jerks or movements	Arm movements
Shoulder shrugs	Hand movements
Arm movements	Writing tics
Hand movements	Dystonic or abnormal postures
Abdominal tensing	Bending or gyrating
Leg, foot, or toe movements	Rotating
	Leg, foot, or toe movements
	Blocking
	Tic-related compulsive behaviors (touching, tapping, grooming, evening-up)
	Copropraxia (obscene gestures)
	Self-abusive behavior
	Groups of simple tics

Simple vocal tics	Complex phonic symptoms
Sounds, noises (coughing, throat clearing, sniffing, or animal or bird noises)	Syllables
	Words
	Coprolalia (obscene words)
	Echolalia (repeating others' words)
	Palilalia (repeating your own words)
	Blocking
	Disinhibited speech

The number of tics, their frequency, duration, intensity, and complexity define tic severity. In mild cases, tics may be restricted to the face, be infrequent, of minimal intensity or complexity, and result in little or no impairment. In more severe cases, tics may involve numerous muscle groups, including the shoulders, arms, legs, and torso; are intense and complex; and result in considerable distress or impairment. Although previously considered to be essential for diagnosis, coprolalia (curse words or socially inappropriate utterances) occurs in only 10–15% of patients (Leckman, King, & Cohen, 1999).

For many, tics are a chronic problem that waxes and wanes, peaking in severity in the early teens, with some improvement in early adulthood (Leckman et al., 1998). Many patients describe an urge or sensation immediately before the occurrence of a tic (Leckman, Walker, & Cohen, 1993). Patients may report that attempts to resist performance of the tic lead to an intensification of this premonitory urge or sensation. Performance of the tic, often to satisfy the premonitory sensation, will at least temporarily quiet the sensation (Himle, Woods, Conelea, Bauer,& Rice, 2007). Indeed, many patients report that tics are performed to satisfy the premonitory sensations (Bliss, 1980; Leckman et al., 1993). The presence of premonitory sensations distinguishes TS from other movement disorders such as Parkinson's disease, Huntington's chorea, and hemiballismus (Scahill, Leckman, & Marek, 1995).

Prevalence of Tic Disorders

Tics are relatively common in children, affecting 12–18% in the school-age population (Scahill, Sukhodolsky, Williams, & Leckman, 2005). Although TS was considered a rare disorder with an estimated prevalence of 1 per 2,000, more recent data from well-designed community surveys suggest that it may be as common as 1–8 children per 1,000 (Costello et al., 1996; Hornse, Banerjee, Zeitlin, & Robertson, 2001). Moreover, if milder forms of the disorder are considered, chronic tic disorder (CTD) prevalence may be as high as 1.5–3% (Scahill et al.).

Co-Occurring Conditions in TS

Those with TS frequently experience co-occurring conditions. Research suggests that approximately 50% of those with TS also have attention-deficit/hyperactivity disorder (ADHD), and 50–90% of persons with TS develop obsessive-compulsive behavior, although only 30–40% develop actual obsessive-compulsive disorder (OCD) (Dedmon, 1990). Individuals with TS also have a higher likelihood of developing depression (Dedmon) and exhibit higher rates of learning disorders, particularly in the areas of mathematics and reading (Burd, Kauffman, & Kerbeshian, 1992).

Impairment Associated With Tic Disorders

The presence of tics can have a negative impact on social, educational, and occupational functioning (Stokes, Bawden, Camfield, Backman, & Dooley, 1991; Sukhodolsky et al., 2003). Children and adults with CTD report problems in dating and maintaining friends (Champion, Fulton, & Shady, 1988) and can be perceived negatively by peers because of the tics (Boudjouk, Woods, Miltenberger, & Long, 2000; Friedrich, Morgan, & Devine, 1996; Woods, Fuqua, & Outman, 1999). Thus, effective treatment strategies to reduce tics may reduce the overall impairment associated with TS. It is also important to note that co-occurring conditions appear to be a better predictor of psychosocial impairment than the tics themselves. As such, clinicians who are treating individuals with multiple diagnoses should consider the negative impact of co-occurring conditions when planning and prioritizing treatment goals.

Diagnostic Criteria for Tic Disorders

In Tables 1.2–1.4, we list the *Diagnostic and Statistical Manual of Mental Disorders, Fourth Edition, Text Revision* (DSM-IV-TR) (American Psychiatric Association, 2000) criteria for TTD, CTD, and TS (called Tourette's disorder in *DSM-IV*).

Table 1.2 Diagnostic Criteria for Transient Tic Disorder

1. Single or multiple motor and/or vocal tics.

2. The tics occur many times a day, nearly every day for at least 4 weeks, but for no longer than 12 consecutive months.

3. The onset is before age 18 years.

4. The disturbance is not due to the direct physiological effects of a substance (e.g., stimulants) or a general medical condition (e.g., Huntington's disease or postviral encephalitis).

5. Criteria have never been met for Tourette's disorder or chronic motor or vocal tic disorder.

Table 1.3 Diagnostic Criteria for Chronic Tic Disorder

1. Single or multiple motor or vocal tics.

2. The tics occur many times a day, nearly every day or intermittently throughout a period of more than 1 year, and during this period, there was never a tic-free period of more than 3 consecutive months.

3. The onset is before age 18 years.

4. The disturbance is not due to the direct physiological effects of a substance (e.g., stimulants) or a general medical condition (e.g., Huntington's disease or postviral encephalitis).

5. Criteria have never been met for Tourette's disorder.

Table 1.4 Diagnostic Criteria for Tourette Syndrome

1. Both multiple motor and one or more vocal tics have been present at some time during the illness, although not necessarily concurrently.

2. The tics occur many times a day (usually in bouts) nearly every day or intermittently throughout a period of more than 1 year, and during this period, there was never a tic-free period of more than 3 consecutive months.

3. The onset is before age 18 years.

4. The disturbance is not due to the direct physiological effects of a substance (e.g., stimulants) or a general medical condition (e.g., Huntington's disease or postviral encephalitis).

Although the current behavioral model has not been fully tested, and the need for further evidence is recognized, it has served as a useful heuristic from which nonpharmacological treatments have been developed and empirically tested. The present model assumes that biological factors are responsible for tic initiation, but behavioral theory is added to describe how the environment may interact with the biology to explain tic variability and how that environment may be modified to promote tic reduction in a therapeutic fashion.

To understand how environmental or contextual factors influence tics, we consider both antecedent and consequent variables. *Antecedents* are those events that happen immediately before tics that make them more or less likely to occur. *Consequences* are those events that occur after tics that make some dimension of those tics (i.e., frequency or intensity) more or less likely to happen in the future. It is also important to note that both antecedents and consequences can be *internal* (occurring inside the patient) or *external* (occurring outside the patient).

External antecedents may include things such as certain settings, specific activities, or the presence of other people. For example, some children may be more likely to tic when others are present, whereas others may be less likely to tic in such a situation. As another example, some children may find that playing sports decreases the likelihood of tics, whereas others may find that coming home from school exacerbates tics.

External consequences may include events such as disruption from an ongoing activity or specific social reactions to the tic. Whereas tics that disrupt ongoing rewarding activities are likely to decrease over time, tics that decrease engagement in aversive activities (e.g., particularly difficult schoolwork) may increase. As another example of external consequences, parents may provide their child with comfort or attention following particularly noticeable tics. In some cases, this attention contingent on tics may make the tics more likely to happen.

Internal antecedents typically involve either the premonitory urges described earlier or broad affective states such as anxiety or boredom.

Anxiety is a factor that is commonly believed to exacerbate tics. Premonitory urges are unpleasant internal experiences that patients with TS report as an "itch," "tickle," "tension," or "tightness" that occurs in either the area specific to the muscles involved in the tic or more globally across the body. Over 90% of persons with TS report the presence of premonitory urges, and those with TS sometimes report that the urges are more problematic than the tics themselves.

Internal consequences primarily involve the reduction of the premonitory urge. When individuals with TS experience the urge and engage in a tic, the urge dissipates or is temporarily relieved (Himle et al., 2007). The reduction of the urge contingent on the tic then reinforces the expression of the tic (i.e., negative reinforcement).

From a behavioral perspective, the effects of both internal and external antecedents and consequences will be unique to the individual. As such, it is important for the clinician to carefully consider all factors when developing behavioral interventions.

Treatment Implications From Integrative Model

Given the aforementioned model, several strategies are used to understand and address the various ways internal or external antecedents or consequences could affect tics. First, to eliminate the potentially negative social consequences of having tics, patient and parent education about tic disorders is conducted. By eliminating such social reactions, those reactions that inadvertently reinforce tics are eliminated and internal antecedent conditions such as anxiety or worry may be diminished, thus potentially eliminating a tic-exacerbating factor. Second, given the fact that anxiety commonly exacerbates tics, relaxation training is provided (Peterson & Azrin, 1992). Third, to understand how contextual variables influence the patient in a unique fashion, function-based assessments are conducted to determine the impact of specific environmental variables on specific tics. These assessment data are then used to construct function-based interventions—individualized approaches patients and parents can use to modify the environment in the service of tic reduction (see Chapter 3 for more details).

Finally, to eliminate the negative reinforcement contingency (i.e., reduction of the urge following the tic), it is necessary to allow the urge to occur, but not be followed by the tic. This results in a reduction of the urge over time, which in turn results in tic reduction. In practice, this requires the clinician to teach the child to become more aware of tic urges and behaviors and engage in a behavior that prevents the completion of the tic. This is accomplished in treatment through HRT. HRT involves awareness training (AT), competing response training, and social support (see Chapter 4 for more details). AT involves teaching the child to be more aware of his or her tics and premonitory urges, and competing response training focuses on teaching the child to engage in a behavior that breaks the link between the premonitory urge or the beginning of the actual tic, and subsequent completion of the tic (e.g., by engaging in an alternate behavior physically incompatible with the tic).

Because the original negative reinforcement contingency still exists in the presence of the premonitory urge, it is important to add additional reinforcement contingencies to increase the probability of the patient engaging in the competing response. There are three ways this is done in HRT. First, in session, the clinician praises the patient's improvement. Second, a social support component is included in HRT and involves having a significant person in the patient's life praise the correct implementation of the competing response (CR). Finally, an inconvenience review component is included, during which the negative aspects of engaging in the tic are brought to the patient's attention so that future reductions in tic frequency are reinforced.

Development of This Treatment Program and Evidence Base

At least 15 research studies have evaluated the efficacy of HRT for TS and other tic disorders (e.g., Azrin & Nunn, 1973; Azrin, Nunn, & Frantz, 1980; Azrin & Peterson, 1988, 1989, 1990; Cloutier, 1985; Deckersbach, Rauch, Buhlmann, & Wilhelm, 2006; Finney, Rapoff, Hall, & Christopherson, 1983; Miltenberger, Fuqua, & McKinley, 1985; O'Connor et al., 2001; Peterson & Azrin, 1992; Wilhelm et al., 2003; Woods, Miltenberger, & Lumley, 1996; Woods & Twohig, 2002;

Woods, Twohig, Flessner, & Roloff, 2003). Many of these involve controlled single-subject research designs. The four published studies employing randomized parallel-group controlled trials were all positive (Azrin & Peterson, 1990; Deckersbach et al., 2006; O'Connor et al., 2001; Wilhelm et al., 2003). Summarizing the literature, Koch and Blacher (2007) noted that the intervention met APA Division 12 criteria as a well-established intervention for tics.

The earliest controlled trials of HRT for tics used no-treatment control groups. To address the limitations of this design, Wilhelm et al. (2003) compared HRT to a supportive psychotherapy (SP) control group. Thirty-two adult TS patients were randomly assigned to 14 sessions of either manualized HRT or SP. Over the course of the treatment, the HRT group showed a significant decline in tic severity (35%; from a mean of 30.5 ± 7.13 at baseline to 19.81 ± 7.58 posttreatment, $p < .01$). This mean posttreatment score was significantly lower than the mean for the SP group (26.88 ± 9.19, $p < .05$). Compared to pretreatment, the HRT patients remained significantly improved at the 10-month follow-up. In a similar study, Deckersbach et al. (2006) randomly assigned 30 adults with TS to supportive therapy or HRT. Following treatment, 10 of the 15 participants in the HRT group were responders, compared to 2 of the 15 in the supportive therapy conditions. These results were maintained at the 6-month follow-up. Combined, results of these and other randomized controlled trials indicate that HRT is an efficacious treatment for TS.

To our knowledge, the only controlled HRT trial for children and adolescents with tics is the recently completed study by Chang and Piacentini (2008) at UCLA. This study used a dismantling design to compare an eight-session (over 10 weeks) manualized HRT protocol (AT plus competing response training) to AT-only in 25 youngsters (21 with TS and 4 with chronic motor tic disorder). Independent evaluators blind to group assignment conducted all outcome assessments. Sample characteristics included the following: mean age = 10.7, 80% male, 48% on stable antitic meds at baseline, 28% comorbid OCD, 20% comorbid ADHD, and mean baseline Yale Global Tic Severity Scale (YGTSS) total score = 24.5 ± 9.5. Both interventions were well accepted and tolerated with 11 of 13 subjects (85%) completing HRT and 9 of 12 (75%)

completing AT. Clinical Global Impression Improvement (CGI-I) ratings of 1 or 2 (Much or Very Much Improved) posttreatment were used to identify treatment responders. Treatment response rates were 46% HRT versus 25% AT (using intent-to-treat) and 55% HRT versus 33% AT (using treatment completers). Although between-group differences failed to reach statistical significance, significant pre–post treatment effects were observed in the HRT group for YGTSS total tics (from 21.4 to 14.9, $p < .01$) for a within-group effect size – .68 (change score – 6.5; $SD = 9.6$). The YGTSS Impairment score also decreased by 60% within the HRT group ($p = .03$) (ES = 2.0). These gains were durable over the short term, with 80% of HRT responders at endpoint remaining so at the 3-month follow-up. In addition to the Chang and Piacentini study, several single-subject experimental designs have been used to evaluate the efficacy of HRT in children, with all showing a positive response. For recent reviews of outcome literature on HRT, see Koch and Blacher (2007) and Himle, Woods, Piacentini, and Walkup (2006).

The Role of Medications

The cornerstone for the short-term reduction of tic severity is medication. Medications are often considered for moderate-to-severe cases of TS, but are used less often for single chronic or motor tics. Clinical trials conducted over the past 25 years provide ample evidence that tics, as well as obsessions and compulsions, hyperactivity, inattention, and impulsiveness, can benefit from targeted pharmacotherapy (for review, see King, Scahill, Lombroso, & Leckman, 2003). Commonly used agents for reducing tic severity include the dopamine-receptor blockers (antipsychotics), and the α_2-agonists. Of the antipsychotics, positive results in the treatment of tics have been observed with haloperidol (Shapiro et al., 1989), pimozide (Bruggeman et al., 2001; Sallee, Nesbitt, Jackson, Sine, & Sethuraman, 1997), and risperidone (Bruggeman et al., 2001; Dion, Annable, Sandor, & Chouinard, 2002; Scahill, Erenberg, & The Tourette Syndrome Practice Parameter Work Group, 2006). Although predictably effective in reducing tics, antipsychotics are associated with a range of adverse effects including sedation, cognitive dulling, weight gain, depression, anxiety, and neurological symptoms (Bruun, 1988). The α-adrenergic receptor agonists are less potent and less consistently effective in reducing tic severity, but they are often preferred over antipsychotics, as they are better tolerated. Many individuals choose not to take medications for their tics or discontinue taking medications because of unwanted side effects. Other individuals find that although their tics are somewhat reduced with medications, they would prefer to have their tics reduced even further. Behavioral treatments for tics can be used with or without adjunct medications.

Overview of Treatment

Behavior therapy for tics as presented in this manual consists of two phases. The first phase consists of eight sessions delivered over the course of 10 weeks. Sessions 1 and 2 are 90 min and the remaining sessions 60 min in duration. The first six sessions are delivered weekly, with 2-week intervals between Sessions 6 and 7 and Sessions 7 and 8. The second phase consists of three booster sessions (Sessions 9–11) held 1, 2, and 3 months after the initial eight sessions have ended. Booster sessions are done to foster increased maintenance and generalization of the treatment.

This manual describes the sequence and required components of all treatment procedures and activities. For children, sessions are conducted jointly with the patient and his or her primary caregiver(s). For older adolescents and adults, sessions are conducted individually, but family members can be invited for education and support. Following is a brief summary of each treatment session.

Session 1: Session 1 focuses on providing the patient and his or her family with a treatment rationale and education about TS, creating a hierarchy of tics to be addressed in treatment, introducing the concept of function-based interventions, establishing a behavioral reward program to enhance motivation (for child patients only), and assigning homework.

Session 2: In Session 2, a review of the difficulties caused by tics is done, function-based interventions and HRT are conducted for the first tic on the hierarchy, and homework is assigned.

Session 3: Session 3 is identical to Session 2, except a new tic is targeted for treatment with HRT and the function-based interventions.

Session 4: In Session 4, function-based treatments and HRT are conducted for the third tic on the hierarchy, the patient is taught relaxed breathing, and homework is assigned.

Session 5: Session 5 involves training the patient in progressive muscle relaxation (PMR). In addition, function-based treatments and HRT are implemented for the fourth tic on the hierarchy. Homework is assigned.

Session 6: In Session 6, function-based interventions and HRT are implemented for the fifth tic on the hierarchy, and relaxation techniques are reviewed. Homework is assigned.

Session 7: Session 7 takes place 2 weeks after Session 6. Session 7 replicates Session 6 and focuses on the sixth tic on the hierarchy. The therapist brings up the topic of relapse prevention. Homework is assigned.

Session 8: Session 8 occurs 2 weeks after Session 7 and represents the end of the initial treatment phase. In this session, treatment procedures are reviewed with the patient and relapse prevention strategies are discussed.

Sessions 9–11 (booster sessions): The booster sessions will begin 4 weeks after Session 8 and will continue for 3 consecutive months. During the booster sessions, no new material is covered, and material covered in the previous treatment sessions is reviewed.

Flexibility in the Implementation of the Manual

The current manual is designed to address one tic per session, over six sessions (i.e., Sessions 2–7). Nevertheless, you should be flexible in the implementation of treatment. If necessary, spend additional sessions working on a particularly difficult tic, or if necessary, go back to a tic that had already been addressed. Although the protocol is designed for 11 sessions, you may need to add additional sessions if the patient has a large number of tics, or if your data show that therapeutic gains have not been maximized.

Therapist Qualifications for Use of This Manual

The manual provides a detailed session-by-session description of the treatment. In our experience, the treatment is best implemented by clinicians familiar with (a) the principles of cognitive-behavior therapy, (b) the TS symptom presentation, and (c) the conditions that frequently co-occur with TS.

Various resources can be used to supplement the training material in this manual. In addition to making use of the Web-based and printed resources listed in the appendix, clinicians are strongly encouraged to attend experiential workshops in which the treatment is described or reviewed, and to seek expert supervision in the procedures.

Patient Characteristics Best Suited for Behavior Therapy for Tics

It is important to note that this treatment was designed specifically to reduce tics. Before treatment, it is important to conduct a comprehensive evaluation to assess for factors that may require more immediate attention. For example, severe attentional difficulties, substance abuse, oppositionality, severe mood disturbance or anxiety, or unstable family environment may need to be addressed before treatment.

Readers are referred to Woods, Piacentini, and Walkup (2007) for a general approach to the clinical management of TS. As Woods et al. note, the clinical management of these more complicated cases may include behavior therapy to treat the tics, but will likely require additional interventions to address the co-occurring issues.

Modifications for Adults

This manual is geared for use with children. Nevertheless, it can be used for adults as well because the core treatment components of function-based environmental modifications, HRT, psychoeducation, and relaxation training are the same for all ages. The treatment components for both children and adults are similar to some extent, with several modifications required for adult patients. When the manual refers to "children and their parents," therapists working with adults should substitute this with "adult patient." Other changes that may need to be made when working with adults are listed here, and specific changes are noted in each session in sections titled, "Working With Adults."

Severity of Tics

Adults with TS may have lived with tics and associated impairments for much longer than children. It is even possible that tics persisting into adulthood represent a more chronic and severe form of the disorder. Because of that, treatment of tics in adults could be more challenging. It is also possible that adults may have already tried various treatments for tics and be skeptical that a brief behavioral treatment will be effective. On the other hand, adults who decide to initiate behavior therapy for their tics may be more motivated for treatment than children, potentially resulting in greater compliance with homework assignments. Furthermore, because this treatment depends in part on an individual's ability to detect sensations that precede tics, adults may have an advantage over children because they usually have better awareness of premonitory urges.

Parental Involvement

Adult patients are usually not accompanied by their parents or significant others for treatment sessions. Parts of the manual that pertain to the parent's role in conducting treatment with children can be safely omitted when working with an adult. When working with older adolescents, therapists should use their clinical judgment regarding the extent of parental involvement in sessions and homework. In our clinical studies, we found it to be helpful, when working with adolescents, to discuss the extent of parental involvement at the beginning of the first session. The majority of families preferred to have a one-on-one format. The therapist may offer to be available to the parents of adolescent patients on an as-needed basis to review treatment progress and to provide education about TS.

Language and Treatment Style

In general, therapists should adopt an age-appropriate language and treatment style with adults. For example, psychoeducation is an important part of treatment. When working with adults, therapists may be able to provide more detailed information and may have to be prepared to answer more advanced questions about TS. Of course, the same is true when talking to parents of children with TS. Like any behavioral intervention, this treatment is a direct, symptom-oriented, and time-limited treatment, which is best conducted in an atmosphere where a patient is comfortable about sharing personal information. Individuals with TS may have different levels of comfort when discussing their tics, and therapists should be empathetic when conducting the initial assessment. Furthermore, TS can cause significant impairment in social life, family relationships, work, and other important areas of life. The emphasis of clinical work with children is on preventing disability, whereas working with adults may require a focus on coping with disability. Therapists should be prepared to respond when presented with very personal accounts of suffering and to provide psychological support while maintaining the focus on the behavioral goals of the treatment manual. Therapists' genuine understanding of the burden and struggle that are part of living with TS will create a foundation for collaborative implementation of this treatment.

Homework

In contrast to the parent-assisted assignments done by the children, homework assignments for adults (i.e., self-monitoring, competing responses, and function-based interventions) are carried out by the patient himself or herself. Likewise, for function-based interventions, adult patients are guided to implement changes themselves (e.g., ask their family to ignore the occurrence of tics during dinner). Note, however, that adult patients, similar to children, can or will choose a support person who may assist in home-based assignments.

Compliance

Although formally equivalent, the content of compliance-enhancing techniques such as the inconvenience review will differ between children and adults. For example, a child may be concerned about students' comments at school, whereas adult patients may worry about the reaction of colleagues at work. For children, this manual describes the implementation of a behavioral reward program, which may or may not be used with adult patients. Adults are often intrinsically motivated, and external rewards typically are not used. If a behavioral program is used, the rewards should be age-appropriate.

Addressing Concerns About Behavior Therapy for TS

During our development and initial presentations of this work, we have run into concerns various professionals and patients have had about using behavior therapy to treat TS. In the sections that follow, we will list each of these issues and briefly describe data supporting their accuracy.

Tic Suppression Strategies Will Backfire

This concern likely comes from observations that many parents report increased tic frequencies in their children upon returning home from school, where they have been "holding in" their tics throughout the day. Nevertheless, three controlled studies have failed to demonstrate this "rebound effect" in tics in children and adolescents with TS, although successful suppression was obtained (Himle & Woods, 2005; Woods & Himle, 2004; Woods et al., 2008). Thus, existing research does not support the idea of a rebound effect following tic suppression. Perhaps these increases at home following school have more to do with contextual changes than "suppression" occurring throughout the day. Future research will be needed to explore this possibility.

Treating One Tic Will Make Untreated Tics Worse

It has been suggested that behavior therapy for tics may exacerbate untreated tics (Burd & Kerbeshian, 1987). However, in a study by Woods et al. (2003), only vocal tics were treated, but motor tics were also measured to see whether there were untoward effects on these symptoms. Results showed that the vocal tics improved and the untreated motor tics did not worsen, suggesting that behavior therapy does not exacerbate untreated tics.

Behavior Therapy Replaces an Old Tic for a New Tic

There is also a persistent belief that symptom substitution occurs when treating tics using behavior therapy. However, research does not support this belief. In studies that have examined the efficacy of behavior therapy, the emergence of new tics as a function of behavior therapy has not been noted (Deckersbach et al., 2006; Wilhelm et al., 2003).

Paying More Attention to Tics Will Make Them Worse

There is a popular belief that focusing one's attention on tics makes them worse (Shimberg, 1995). There is also a belief among many who treat those with TS that talking about tics makes them worse (Marcks et al., 2004). Although it is true that for some individuals a general increase in focus on their tics may produce a temporary tic exacerbation, data do not support the assertion that increasing attention on tics *in the context of treatment* has any detrimental effects (Woods et al., 1996). For this reason, we generally tell parents to ignore the tics, but to pay attention to how well the child is doing his or her therapeutic exercises.

Using the Patient Workbooks

As with any behavior therapy, the successful completion of homework and full participation in treatment is vital. To aid in the assignment and completion of homework, and to encourage full participation, patient workbooks have been created. There is one workbook geared toward children and their parents, and another designed specifically for adults. The workbooks contain all necessary materials to help patients successfully complete treatment. Specific forms include all necessary self-monitoring forms, forms to facilitate the implementation of HRT and function-based treatment recommendations both in and out of sessions, and psychoeducational materials that can be read at the patient's leisure.

Structure of the Manual

The current manual is organized for maximum utility. Chapter 2 describes a comprehensive approach to the assessment of those with tic disorders. Chapters 3 and 4 describe the steps involved in two procedures that cut across nearly all sessions. In Chapter 3 function-based assessment and interventions are discussed. Chapter 4 talks about HRT. Following these chapters, the guide offers a session-by-session description of how to implement treatment, referring back to Chapters 3 and 4 when necessary and presenting new session-specific material as needed.

Chapter 2 | *Assessment Strategies for Tourette Syndrome*

Tourette syndrome can be a complex disorder with many nuances that inevitably lends itself best to an individualized assessment and treatment approach. A comprehensive assessment of tic disorder should involve a thorough examination across several domains, including diagnosis or differential diagnosis, assessment of tic symptoms, evaluation of comorbid conditions, description of functional impact, and past treatment history, including both psychopharmacological and psychosocial interventions (Woods, Piacentini, & Himle, 2007). Assessment of tics is often complicated by the reactive quality and waxing and waning nature of symptoms. Accurate establishment of baseline tic severity and response to treatment typically requires the use of a combination of standardized clinician-administered and patient or informant self-reports. A complete discussion of the assessment of tic severity, related functional impairments, and comorbid symptomatology is beyond the scope of this manual. However, several additional sources of information on this topic are available, including Woods et al. and Leckman and Cohen (1999b).

Diagnosis or Differential Diagnosis

Clinical interviews and observations are the primary tools used to establish a diagnosis given the current absence of a medical test for diagnosing TS. Although discriminating between the various tic disorders can be relatively straightforward, it may be more difficult to distinguish tic disorders from other movement disorders, allergies, or related psychiatric disturbances in which repetitive movements are common. Movement disorders that present with symptomology similar to TS include myoclonus, dystonia, Sydenham or Huntington Chorea, stereotypic movement disorder, and restless legs syndrome. Individuals with a questionable presentation—indicated by late onset with no prior tic history, by the absence of current or past facial tics and of tics that do not wax or wane, by the presence of tics that fail to shift in bodily location and of complex tics without a history of simple tics—warrant referral to an experienced medical specialist to rule out any underlying medical explanation for the symptoms under consideration. A preliminary medical evaluation may also be helpful in ruling out other possible explanations for tics. For example, throat clearing or sniffing tics may be related to allergies. Eye squinting or blinking tics may be a symptom of an underlying eye problem (e.g., poor vision or infection). Furthermore, any physical consequences of frequent tic expression (e.g., muscle strain or soreness) may be assessed and addressed during an initial medical exam.

The differentiation between symptoms of tic disorders and repetitive movements associated with stereotypic movement disorders and OCD often lies in a gray area. In distinguishing between tics and stereotypic movement conditions, it is helpful to assess whether the patient has a developmental disability as it is likely that repetitive behaviors (e.g., hand flapping or body rocking) in this patient population are more indicative of a stereotypic movement versus a tic disorder. In addition, a single complex repetitive movement that does not vary in anatomical location or wax and wane in severity, along with an absence of a history of more simple tics, may be more related to a diagnosis of stereotypic movement disorder.

With regard to differentiating between a complex tic and an OCD-related compulsion, it may be helpful to assess whether physical anxiety or specific cognitive content precedes the repetitive behavior given that an OCD compulsion is more likely to be associated with such phenomena. Additionally, complex tics are more likely to be related to a vague urge or physical tension preceding the repetitive behavior than OCD compulsions.

Assessment of Tic Symptoms

Overall tic symptom severity should reflect the multiple dimensions upon which tics can vary: topography, number, frequency, complexity, noticeability, intensity, interference, subjective distress, and temporal stability (i.e., waxing and waning). Such a multifactorial approach allows the clinician to consider how each dimension contributes uniquely to an individual's disorder. For example, a patient with a single, infrequent, painful tic who has been socially excluded may report much more distress than an individual with several face and body tics that occur frequently with less intensity and noticeability. A thorough assessment of tics should be conducted using the following assessment modalities.

Clinical Interviews

One of the most useful strategies for assessing tic disorders is the clinical interview. A patient interview, supplemented with interviews from other relevant sources (e.g., spouse, parent, teachers, and family), is the best approach. Although a detailed unstructured interview can often provide much of the necessary information, an examiner may find it useful to supplement his or her assessment with one of several available semistructured and/or structured clinical interviews (e.g., Leckman, King, & Cohen, 1999; Woods et al., 2007).

The first step in the interview process is to gather information about the onset and course of symptoms. It is useful to know the age of onset as well as descriptive information regarding the topography, frequency, intensity, and stability of initial tics. Tics commonly emerge in a head-down pattern, and simple tics (e.g., eye-blinking) usually appear before complex tics (if complex tics are present). In addition, it is not uncommon for initial tics to be transient, with prolonged periods during which the tics are absent or are not noticed.

Semistructured clinical interviews are often used to aid the examiner in obtaining symptom information and quantifying the severity of tics. Perhaps the most widely used instrument is the Yale Global Tic Severity Scale (YGTSS) (Leckman et al., 1989). The YGTSS is a clinician-administered, semistructured interview that can be administered relatively quickly (approximately 15–30 min). Throughout the interview, the examiner gathers information separately for motor and phonic tics. The YGTSS consists of three main components: a symptom checklist, tic severity ratings, and an assessment of impairment. The checklist segment of the YGTSS includes an extensive list of tic topographies most commonly endorsed by individuals with tic symptoms. The tic severity ratings of the YGTSS are composed of assessments in various dimensions including the number of tics, frequency of tics, intensity or noticeability of tics, complexity or purposefulness of tics, and degree to which tics interrupt or interfere with intended actions. Each dimension is rated on a 0–5-point scale, and motor and phonic tics are rated separately. The motor and phonic tic dimensional ratings are summed to provide a total tic severity score ranging from 0 to 50. In addition to the dimensional ratings, the YGTSS provides an overall rating of impairment. The overall impairment rating is a score ranging from 0 (no impairment) to 50 (severe impairment causing severe disability and distress). The total severity and impairment ratings are interpreted separately from one another.

Self- or Informant-Report Inventories

These measures are usually easy to administer, especially over repeated administrations. The disadvantage is that most provide information only on a limited number of dimensions (e.g., number and frequency). The Parent Tic Questionnaire (PTQ) is a brief self-report measure that instructs parents to rate the presence or absence of 14 motor and 14 vocal tics in their child, along with the frequency, intensity, and controllability of the tics (Chang, Himle, Tucker, Woods, & Piacentini, 2008). Although a relatively new measure, initial reports suggest the PTQ demonstrates good reliability and validity. The Adult Tic Questionnaire (ATQ) is a recently developed self-report rating scale, parallel in format and content to the PTQ (Chang et al.).

Assessment of Premonitory Sensations

Many individuals with TS report unpleasant, and sometimes distressing, cognitions or somatosensory events before performing a tic (traditionally referred to as "premonitory urges"). These private events are often reported through detailed descriptions of the experience ("it feels like energy [or tension, a tickle, an itch, etc.]") or vague descriptions ("it feels like something just isn't right"). Most often, premonitory urges are temporarily lessened contingent upon the performance of the tic and can occur at the specific site of the tic or globally throughout large regions of the body. Assessment of pre-tic phenomena is important for a few reasons. First, these sensations can often be uncomfortable and disturbing to the patient and as such should be treated as a symptom of the disorder. Second, awareness of pre-tic thoughts or sensations may be important for treatment planning. Third, complex tics that are preceded by vague cognitive experiences are often difficult to differentiate from symptoms of OCD. A detailed assessment of cognitive antecedents will help the examiner to ensure an appropriate diagnosis.

Assessment of premonitory phenomena is usually accomplished during the clinical interview. In our experience, older patients and individuals who have suffered from the disorder for longer periods of time are usually quite adept at describing their pre-tic sensations. Younger and less experienced individuals, however, can often benefit from the use of standardized descriptive phrases. The Premonitory Urge for Tics Scale (PUTS) is a brief nine-item self-report measure that asks individuals to rate several premonitory urge descriptions on a 0–4-point ordinal scale anchored by "not at all true" and "very true" (Woods, Piacentini, Himle, & Chang, 2005). In addition to acquiring descriptive information, it may be useful to obtain information about the location and intensity of premonitory urges. This can be accomplished by having the patient indicate the location of pre-tic sensations using depictions of human figures (both dorsal and ventral views) (Leckman et al., 1993).

Assessment of Comorbid Conditions

Owing to the high prevalence of conditions comorbid with TS, an assessment of TS should include measures sufficiently sensitive to detect coexisting psychopathology of sufficient severity to adversely impact treatment of tics and/or warrant separate intervention. Perhaps the most difficult differential diagnosis is that of TS and OCD. As mentioned earlier, complex tics often closely resemble the ritualistic behavior exhibited by individuals with OCD. In addition, vague premonitory urges (especially those described in cognitive terms) often resemble obsessions.

In our experience, the best approach is a two-step process. First, establish the presence of TS. As noted earlier, complex, seemingly ritualistic tics are rarely the only tics present and are typically evident later in the developmental progression of the disorder. Second, evaluate the relationship between the preritualistic cognitions and the repetitive behavior of concern. By definition, compulsive acts are performed to alleviate, reduce, or avoid anxiety associated with the obsessions, whereas the cognitive events that precede complex tics, although alleviated by the tic, rarely directly produce anxiety. The Yale-Brown Obsessive Compulsive Scale (YBOCS) (Goodman et al., 1989a, 1989b) and parallel Child YBOCS (Scahill et al., 1997) are reliable and valid semistructured clinical interviews assessing OCD severity and change over time. The interviews contain separate sections for obsessions and compulsions, and each section includes a checklist of symptoms as well as items to rate frequency or duration, interference, distress, resistance, and control related to OCD symptoms. Separate scores, ranging from 0 to 20, are obtained for obsessions and compulsions, with a combined total of 0–40. A score of 16 is often used to indicate clinically significant OCD.

Various parent- and child-report rating scales can be used to efficiently and reliably screen for the presence of comorbid problems. The Child Behavior Checklist (CBCL), an 118-item parent-report measure of child psychopathology, is one of the most extensively tested and normed rating scales available and possesses excellent psychometrics. T-scores allow for normative comparisons across three broadband factors (social competence, and internalizing and externalizing behavior problems) and 11 narrowband subscales (Achenbach, 1991).

Other scales providing a more focused evaluation of common comorbidities in children and adolescents include the following:

> ADHD Rating Scale (ADHD-RS). The ADHD-RS is an 18-item scale derived from the ADHD criteria in *DSM-IV* (DuPaul, Power, Anastopoulos, & Reid, 1998) and can be used to aid in the diagnosis of ADHD in children and monitor treatment effects (Scahill et al., 2001).

> Children's Depression Inventory (CDI). The CDI is a 27-item (rated 0–2) child self-report questionnaire assessing depressive symptomatology over the preceding 2 weeks. Age- and

gender-based T-scores are generated for five factors: negative mood, interpersonal problems, ineffectiveness, anhedonia, and negative self-esteem. Reliability and concurrent validity have been found to be high, and age- and gender-based norms are available (Kovacs, 1992).

- Multidimensional Anxiety Scale for Children (MASC). The MASC is a 39-item 4-point Likert self-report rating scale of child anxiety symptoms. The measure bears reasonable correspondence to the *DSM-IV* anxiety disorder diagnostic categories for children and adolescents. The MASC possesses excellent test–retest reliability, internal consistency, and validity, and is scored against nationally derived normative data (March, Parker, Sullivan, Stallings, & Conners, 1997).

For adults, the following self-report measures may be useful:

- Conners' Adult ADHD-RS (CAARS) (Conners, Erhardt, & Sparrow, 1999). The CAARS comprises 18 items (rated on a 4-point scale), each of which corresponds to one of the 18 *DSM-IV* symptoms for ADHD.

- Beck Depression Inventory-II (BDI-II) (Beck & Steer, 1987). The BDI-II is a well-established 21-item self-report measure that assesses the severity of depressive symptoms during the past 2 weeks. The BDI-II is quick, efficient, and provides both clinical and nonclinical norms.

- Beck Anxiety Inventory (BAI) (Beck & Steer, 1993). The BAI is also a well-validated and easy to use 21-item self-report measure of anxiety symptoms. Similar to the BDI-II, extensive normative data are available for the BAI.

Assessment of Current Functioning

In addition to tic symptoms, it is important to assess how well a patient is functioning with his or her disorder. Research has shown that those with TS may be viewed as less acceptable than their peers (Boudjouk, Woods, Miltenberger, & Long, 2000), experience greater levels of unemployment (Shady, Broder, Staley, & Furer, 1995), and decreased overall quality of life (Elstner, Selai, Trimble, & Robertson, 2001). Although not as well studied in children as adults, youngsters with tic disorder have also been shown to experience increased rates of psychosocial impairment and stress compared with controls with psychosocial stress, predicting increased tic severity over a 2-year follow-up period (Lin et al., 2007).

Given that the ultimate goal of most treatment interventions is normalization of psychosocial functioning, systematic evaluation of the level of functional impairment at baseline and throughout treatment is an important consideration. For children, this would include an assessment of social, academic, and home or family functioning. For adolescents and adults, this assessment would also include evaluation of current and past substance use and/or abuse, along with occupational and relationship or sexual functioning.

In addition to the Yale Global Tic Severity Scale Impairment rating, which is appropriate for both children and adults, the Child Behavior Checklist Social Competence ratings provide a reasonable measure of functional impairment for children and adolescents up to age 18. In addition, the following two measures provide quick and reliable ratings of functional status or life satisfaction in adults:

> The Sheehan Disability Inventory (Leon, Shear, Portera, & Klerman, 1992) is a 4-item self-report scale that assesses work, social, and family disability on 10-point scales. The ratings from these items are then integrated into a single 5-point scale rating ranging from no symptoms (1) to symptoms that radically change or prevent normal work or social life (5).

> The Schwartz Outcome Scale (SOS-10) (Blais et al., 1999) consists of 10 items assessing general life satisfaction (e.g. "I am generally satisfied with my psychological health"). Each item is rated on a 6-point rating scale from "never" (0) to "all the time or nearly all the time" (6), resulting in a possible range of scores between 0 and 60.

Chapter 3   *Function-Based Intervention*

Principles of Function-Based Intervention

A core component of comprehensive behavioral intervention for tics (CBIT) is the function-based intervention. The purpose of function-based interventions is to isolate the factors that make tics worse for the patient and modify those factors to bring about tic reduction and decreased impairment.

Factors that can make tics worse or lead to poorer functional outcomes can be categorized into antecedents and consequences. *Antecedents* are those internal or external events that occur before tics. Examples of *internal* antecedent events include anxiety, anticipation, excitement, anger, etc. Examples of *external* antecedent events include particular settings (e.g., in front of others), certain classes (e.g., math and gym), watching television, the presence of particular people, etc. *Consequences* are those events that occur in reaction to tics. Examples include a child being asked to leave a situation because of her tics, social reactions such as sibling or peer teasing, or the comforting of parents after a child has a particularly noticeable tic.

Function-based interventions are conducted on a tic-by-tic basis. In the current protocol, we implement HRT and function-based interventions for each tic targeted in treatment. To choose effective function-based interventions, a two-stage process is followed. Both stages are conducted and/or reviewed in each of Sessions 2–11. The first stage involves isolating the contextual variables responsible for tic exacerbation and negative life impact related to the tics. This stage is called the *function-based assessment*. The second stage involves *selecting the function-based interventions* depending on the results of the assessment.

Two methods are used to assess the variables that make tics worse. The first is a structured functional assessment interview conducted between you, the patient, and her parent(s). The second is a Functional Assessment Self-Report Form for the patient or parents (found in the workbook) that can be used between sessions. To help you conduct the assessment interview, you will use the Functional Assessment Form (FAF). Blank FAFs (Child and Adult Versions) are provided at the end of the chapter. If you need additional copies, you may photocopy them from the book. The completed form(s) should be retained for future sessions.

To complete the FAF, write down the first tic being treated in the first row of the form and ask about the antecedents listed. Specifically, ask whether the tic seems to be worse (e.g., more frequent and more intense) in that particular situation. For each new antecedent endorsed by the parents or patient, use a new number to note the antecedent in the corresponding column on the FAF (i.e., 1 for first antecedent endorsed, 2 for second antecedent endorsed, etc.). After reviewing the antecedents listed on the FAF, ask whether there are any *other* situations, people, or places where motor tics occur more frequently than usual. If so, ask the patient to describe those situations. If the description is sufficiently different from what has already been checked, write down a description of the new antecedent in one of the "other" boxes and assign the next number of the antecedent sequence (1, 2, 3 . . .) in the corresponding box. Continue with this process until the patient and parents have exhausted all antecedents for the tic currently being discussed.

After completing the antecedent section, review with the patient the consequences for tics occurring in each of the settings. You may use the following sample dialogue:

You mentioned to me that your "tic" really seems to happen a lot in (state the antecedent marked with 1 on the FAF). *I'd like to ask you about what happens while you tic or right after you tic in that situation (or around that person or in that place).*

Ask about the specific consequences listed on the FAF and put the number (1, 2, 3 . . .) of each relevant antecedent under the consequences that are present for that antecedent. After reviewing with the patient the consequences listed, ask whether there are any other things that happen or that people do or say during or after the patient tics in this situation. If the description is sufficiently different from what has already been checked, write down a description of the new consequence in one of the "other" boxes and assign the appropriate number (1, 2, 3 . . .) in the corresponding box. Continue with this process until the patient and parents have exhausted all consequences for all antecedents.

See Figure 3.1 for an example of a completed child version of the FAF. The example shows a patient (Billy) with three tics: a complex motor tic involving the rapid bringing together of the knees followed by a neck extension with the head thrown back (leg or head tic), a simple vocal tic involving a small rapid cough, and a simple eye-blinking tic. During the interview, it became clear that the complex tic was likely to occur frequently at home after school and while watching TV or playing video games. When the complex tic occurred at home after school, Billy's mother comforted him, and his younger sister laughed at him. When it occurred while he watched TV, his brother would tell him to stop it, and he got to stay up later so that he could "calm down" before going to bed. His coughing tic was likely to happen in the classroom, while playing sports in gym class, and when he was anxious. When he was anxious, Billy had particular thoughts about being evaluated negatively by his peers. In all of these situations, his teachers told him to "knock it off," and his peers laughed at him. His eye-blinking tic was most common in the classroom, late at night around bedtime, and while doing homework. However, he reported no obvious consequences for his eye-blinking tic in any situation.

In addition to the functional assessment interview, it may be useful to have the patient and/or parents monitor potentially important variables over the next week using the Functional Assessment Self-Report Form in the workbook. Data obtained through functional assessment interview can be supplemented using the results of the patient's self-report.

Date completed: 2/24/08

Child: Billy

Tic (From Hierarchy)	Leg/Head Tic	Coughing	Blinking						
ANTECEDENTS									
Classroom		1	1						
At Home After School	1								
Public Place Other Than School									
Watching TV/Video Games	2								
Playing Sports		2							
During Meals									
Bedtime			2						
Doing Homework			3						
In Car									
Other Anxiety -Thoughts about people judging him		3							
Other_____									
Other_____									
CONSEQUENCES									
Parent Tells Child to Stop Tics									
Teacher/Other Adult Tells Child To Stop		1,2,3							
Peer/Sibling Tells Child to Stop	2								
Parent/Teacher/Sibling Comforts Child	1								
Someone Laughs at or With the Child	1	1,2,3							
Child is Asked to Leave the Area									
Child Doesn't Complete Meal, Homework, or School Task									
Child Gets to Stay up Later	2								
Child Doesn't Have to do Chores or Other Required Activity									
Other_____									
Other_____									
Other_____									

Figure 3.1

Example of Completed Functional Assessment Form (FAF)—Child Version

Functional Assessment Treatment Recommendations

After completing the functional assessment interview and reviewing the functional analysis data, you and the patient or parents will develop specific function-based treatment recommendations with the aid of the interventions listed in the section that follows. Because some antecedent situations are common to tic disorders, some specific interventions have been developed, and these are listed next. Have the patient and/or parents record the details of the treatment plan on the Function-Based Interventions Form in the workbook. A separate function-based treatment recommendation should be made for each specific antecedent.

Sample Function-Based Interventions

Antecedent Interventions

Classroom Tics

1. Inform the child's classroom teachers that the child has TS and explain the uncontrollability of the child's condition.

2. The child should be seated in a location that diminishes noticeability of tics, but still includes the child in the classroom experience.

3. Identify and simplify difficult tasks that exacerbate tics (e.g., do work at home if possible or break larger tasks into smaller tasks).

After School Tics

1. Provide the child 15 min of free time in her room when she returns from school before making any specific requests of the child.

2. After 15 min, regardless of tic status, the child should return to general family living areas and practice therapy-relevant exercises.

Public Place Other Than School

1. Provide the child with an explanation she can use to explain tics and their uncontrollable nature for individuals who ask or who are teasing the child.

2. Before entering the situation, the parent should prompt the appropriate use of the competing response (CR).

3. Parents and children should avoid unnecessary or socially irrelevant high-risk situations.

Watching TV or Playing Video Games

1. Limit the amount of time in front of TV.

2. When the child watches TV, the parent should be available to provide social support.

Tics While Playing Sports

1. Educate the child's coaches and teammates that the child has TS and explain the uncontrollability of the child's condition.

During Meals

1. Eliminate all tic-exacerbating activities or stimuli at least 30 min before mealtime.

2. Provide child with a 15-min "meal warning."

Bedtime Tics

1. Establish a specific bedtime routine that is adhered to regularly.

2. Eliminate all other tic exacerbating stimuli at least 30 min before bedtime (e.g., turn off TV and have homework completed).

3. Have the child engage in relaxation practice 15 min before bed.

In-Car Tics

1. Seat the child in a place in the car where tics will cause the least safety risk (e.g., middle of the back seat).

2. Remind the child that the car is a good place to practice her CR exercises.

3. Car trips should be scheduled during times of day when tics are less likely to happen.

Consequence Interventions
If Social Attention Is Endorsed

1. Parents/siblings/teachers/peers/coaches should no longer tell the child to stop the target tic.

2. Parents/siblings/teachers/peers/coaches should no longer comfort the child when the target tic occurs.

3. Parents/siblings/teachers/peers/coaches should no longer laugh at the child when the target tic occurs.

4. Parents/teachers/coaches should provide specific instructions to peers not to react to the tics; parents should remind nonstrangers not to react to the tics or comfort the child.

5. If the child is being teased or asked about the tics, the parent should not answer for the child, but should let her provide the explanation.

If Escape Items Are Endorsed

1. The child should not be encouraged to leave the room for mild tics; however, if the tics are distracting to the remaining children, the child should have a predetermined "safe" place to tic, but should always bring her work along and complete all assigned work.

2. The child should be allowed to request a break if she feels disruptive tics beginning to occur, but must bring along and complete all assigned work.

3. Must begin homework after 30 min at home, should work until finished, and should get a 5-min break for every 30 min.

4. Parents should prompt tic management strategies, but should not necessarily have the child leave the situation.

5. If the situation demands the child leave, the parent should identify a safe place for the child to tic, and the child should be given the opportunity to exhibit tic-control strategies.

6. Parents should prompt the use of the CR.

7. Parents should not send the child out of the TV room, but should consider turning TV off and providing child with opportunity to practice tic management strategies.

8. Do not allow the child to skip a turn or sit the child down because of the tics.

9. The child should not be sent from the table.

10. The child should be encouraged to practice tic management strategies.

11. The child must not be allowed to come out of room after assigned bedtime. If the child complains of not being able to sleep, she should be asked to stay in her room without doing entertaining events. She should be encouraged to practice tic-control treatments at this time.

12. Parents should make every effort to get the child to the determined destination, arranging alternative means of transportation if necessary or possible.

13. If the child is doing a task in the car, she should be required to complete the task, even if it is done after the car trip has been completed.

Use the existing function-based interventions as applicable, making them relevant to the patient's particular situation. If an applicable intervention for your patient's circumstances is not listed, you will need to develop one of your own. Keep the following five principles in mind when developing function-based interventions.

1. When possible, situations or settings that make the tic more likely to happen should be either minimized or eliminated.

2. In situations where tics are more likely to happen, events that occur soon after a tic happens should be eliminated if possible. Examples of events that may be eliminated include excusing the child from a difficult situation, commenting on tics, or comforting or consoling the patient after tics happen.

3. When entering those situations where tics are more likely to happen, part of the function-based intervention should involve reminding the patient to use the HRT strategies taught for that particular tic.

4. When entering situations that are not easily modifiable, the patient should learn strategies to minimize her own reactions that may contribute to tics. For example, if anxiety makes tics worse, it will likely be difficult to prevent all anxiety-producing events from occurring. In such a case, interventions may focus on teaching the patient ways to modify her anxious response to such situations. Examples of such interventions could include challenging and replacing anxiogenic cognitions and teaching the child to relax in such situations.

5. The final rule when developing function-based interventions is to minimize the impact of tics on the child. Educating teasing peers about the child's condition and providing specific instructions about how to react appropriately to the tics (i.e., without negative affect, disgust, shock, etc.) are examples of such an intervention.

After developing the function-based intervention for a particular tic, write it down (or have the patient or parents record it) on the Function-Based Interventions Form in the workbook. Develop a concrete plan with the parents or patient to implement the agreed-upon intervention. Troubleshoot these interventions when necessary. A sample Function-Based Interventions Form for Billy (the patient discussed previously) is shown in Figure 3.2.

Child: Billy

Date Developed: 2/24/08 Date Implemented: 2/25/08

Target Tic: Leg/head tic

List specific plausible strategies that can prevent the antecedent situations from occurring or prevent the child from encountering them.

1. Provide Billy 15 minutes of free time in his room when he returns from school before making any specific requests of him.

2. After 15 minutes, Billy will return to general family living areas and practice therapy-relevant exercises.

List specific strategies that could make a situation less likely to make tics worse if the situation cannot be prevented.

1. Limit Billy's time watching TV to no more than 15 consecutive minutes before he is required to get up and do something else for approximately 5 minutes. Limit TV-watching to no more than 30 minutes per day.

2. When Billy watches TV, his parents should be available to provide social support in completing competing response exercises.

If social attention (telling to stop, comforting, laughing at) was a consequence endorsed for this tic, list ways in which this attention can no longer be delivered.

1. Parents/siblings/teachers/peers/coaches should no longer tell Billy to stop the leg/head tic.

2. Parents/siblings/teachers/peers/coaches should no longer comfort Billy when the leg/head tic occurs.

3. Parents/siblings/teachers/peers/coaches should no longer laugh at Billy when the target tic occurs.

4. Parents should set up a meeting with Billy's teacher in the next week to review these treatment guidelines.

Figure 3.2

Example of Completed Function-Based Interventions Form

Functional Assessment Form (FAF)—Child Version

Patient: _____ Date completed: _____

Tic (From Hierarchy)										
ANTECEDENTS										
Classroom										
At Home After School										
Public Place Other Than School										
Watching TV/Video Games										
Playing Sports										
During Meals										
Bedtime										
Doing Homework										
In Car										
Other Anxiety -Thoughts about people judging him										
Other_____										
Other_____										
CONSEQUENCES										
Parent Tells Child to Stop Tics										
Teacher/Other Adult Tells Child To Stop										
Peer/Sibling Tells Child to Stop										
Parent/Teacher/Sibling Comforts Child										
Someone Laughs at or With the Child										
Child is Asked to Leave the Area										
Child Doesn't Complete Meal, Homework, or School Task										
Child Gets to Stay up Later										
Child Doesn't Have to do Chores or Other Required Activity										
Other_____										
Other_____										
Other_____										

Tic (From Hierarchy)									
ANTECEDENTS									
Work									
At Home After Work									
Public Place Other Than Work									
Watching TV									
Exercising/Working Out									
During Meals									
Bedtime or Morning Routine (circle appropriate)									
On computer									
In Car									
Anticipation or Waiting for Something to Happen									
Around a Specific Person_____									
Interrupted Behavior (specify)_____									
Other_____									
CONSEQUENCES									
Support Person/Friend/Other Person Tells Patient to Stop Tics									
Support Person/Friend/Other Person Leaves the Area									
Support Person/Friend/Other Person Comforts the Patient									
Someone Laughs at or With the Patient									
Someone Expresses Annoyance with the Patient									
Patient is Asked to Leave the Area									
Patient Doesn't Complete Activity of Task									
Patient Spends Time Doing Pleasurable Activities									
Patient Gets Help with Unwanted Chore or Activity									
Other_____									

Functional Assessment Form (FAF)—Adult Version

Patient: _____

Date completed: _____

Chapter 4 *Habit Reversal Training*

The habit reversal training (HRT) portion of treatment consists of the following procedures: awareness training, competing response (CR) training, and social support. All three procedures are implemented for each tic targeted in treatment. The purpose of HRT is to make the patient aware of when the tic is happening or is about to happen (awareness training), teach the patient to engage in a behavior that is physically incompatible with the tic (CR training), and find someone (typically a parent for a child patient) who can reinforce the patient for using the CR correctly and prompt the patient to use the CR when the patient does not recognize that a tic has occurred.

In the sections that follow, we describe how to implement HRT. The HRT protocol described in this chapter is replicated in Sessions 2–8, with a new tic targeted in each session. Although it is important to implement the procedure as written for the first tic or two, as patients become more accustomed to the process, implementation may become more streamlined. Through repeated practice of HRT procedures for the patient's various tics, it is expected that the patient will become adept at recognizing new tics, developing new CRs, and implementing them appropriately as needed.

Awareness Training

The purpose of awareness training is to teach the patient to verbally acknowledge when tics happen and are about to happen. Awareness training is seen as an important process in HRT. For any targeted tics, do not proceed with CR training and social support until an adequate awareness can be achieved for that tic. Awareness training involves the following four steps:

1. Introducing awareness

2. Describing the tic

3. Describing the antecedent sensations and behaviors

4. Acknowledging antecedent sensations and the occurrence of tics

Introduction of Awareness Training

Awareness training is done to teach the patient to acknowledge each tic and its premonitory sensations. This is important because if the patient is unaware of the tic or premonitory urges (when present), the procedure likely will be ineffective.

Provide a rationale before starting awareness training.

> *Now we're going to practice becoming aware of when you do your tic. We want to make you more aware of when your tic is happening, because the rest of the treatment depends on you being able to tell a tic is happening or about to happen. This is very important, because if you want to learn to manage something, you first have to know when it is happening. We'll do a number of exercises so that by the time you leave today, you will know when your tic is happening or about to happen.*

After the rationale, work with the patient to define the tic along with pre-tic sensations and behaviors. To promote awareness, have the patient point out actual or simulated examples of his tic, while providing prompts and feedback. Each of these specific procedures is outlined in the following sections.

Describing the Tic

The patient should describe the tic in great detail. This may involve looking at exactly which muscles are moving, or how the patient's limbs move to perform the tic. For example, if the patient lifts his head and stretches his neck during a neck jerking tic, the head lifting and neck

#	Name of tic	Definition	Tic signals	Competing response
1	Leg/head tic	Calves tighten, heels come up, knees come together forcefully making a cracking noise. As the knees come together, the chin goes down toward the chest and then goes up toward the sky as the top of the head goes back.	General tense feelings in the legs and neck Calves tighten Heels go up	Place heels flat on the ground, hold knees together and tighten thighs while tensing neck muscles gently

Figure 4.1

Example of Completed Tics, Tic Signals, and Competing Responses Form

stretching should be included in the description. An example of such a definition is described in the sample Tics, Tic Signals, and Competing Responses form (see Figure 4.1). If the patient fails to describe a key feature of the tic, you should point this out. An example of how this procedure could be introduced follows.

> *We first need to be on the same page about what we're dealing with. Let's get a really good description of your tic. Use as much detail as you can. What does it sound like? Look like? Is it fast or slow? Is it noticeable or not? Are there different parts to it, or is it just one movement?*

After the definition is created, have the patient describe the sensations and behaviors that precede the tic.

Describing Antecedent Sensations and Behaviors

The purpose of this procedure is to have the patient recognize antecedent sensations and behaviors that may inform him that the tic is about to occur. These sensations and behaviors should be called "warning signs," or "tic signals," and the topic could be introduced as follows.

If you are really going to treat a problem like tics, you need to be aware of them as they happen or are about to happen. The first part of being aware is being able to define the problem. The second part is actually being able to say when they happen or are about to happen. In the case of tics, your body is probably giving you signals that let you know tics are about to happen. I'd like you to think about the signals your body is giving you that let you know the tic is about to occur. These signals can either be things you do or things you feel.

Individuals with tics may have behaviors and private experiences that lead up to the actual tic (i.e., premonitory urges). Examples of private experiences include an uncomfortable, vague itching sensation, tightness, tension, or something as vague as "it just feels like I need to do it." Specific overt behaviors preceding tics, or tics occurring early in the complex tic chain, may also function as warning signs. For example, if a person has an arm extending tic, he may raise his arms from his side before the tic. In this case, the warning sign (raising arms) is public. Work with the patient to establish all tic signals he may experience and write them down on the Tics, Tic Signals, and Competing Responses form under the column "Tic Signals" (see Figure 4.1 for an example). If the patient claims there are no warning signs (which may occur commonly in children), point out a few of the examples listed in this section and ask the patient whether any apply to him. If the patient still denies the presence of warning signs, ask him to try to be aware of any sign upon engaging in tics, and proceed to the next awareness training procedure—acknowledging self-tics.

Acknowledging Self-Tics

Following a comprehensive description of the tic and its signals, have the patient point out when they happen. When asking the patient to detect his own tics, it is possible that he will not do the tics. If this occurs, either find a situation that is likely to worsen the tic, leave the room and watch from behind a one-way mirror, or have the patient simulate his own tic and warning signs. Tic simulation, while not ideal, may be helpful in having the patient begin to establish the link between tics and acknowledgement of them. The procedure can be introduced to the patient as follows.

> *Now we're going to practice having you notice your tic. We're going to talk about various topics for the next few minutes or so. During this time, I want you to raise an index finger every time you have (name the tic). Do this as soon as the tic happens.*

Praise the patient when he accurately recognizes a tic and provide feedback and repeat the instructions when the patient fails to acknowledge a tic that has occurred. Continue this process until the patient has correctly acknowledged four of five tics *or* until you are confident the patient is aware of the tics. Next, ask the patient to replicate the procedure, this time trying to detect his own warning signs instead of the tic itself.

> *Next, we're going to practice being aware of your tic signals. I'd like you to do the same thing with your tic signals. We're going to talk about different things again for a few minutes, and I want you to lift an index finger when you notice one of your signals. Do this as soon as you notice one.*

The signals may not occur. If this happens, ask the patient to simulate the tic signals and acknowledge them.

Let the patient know that making him more aware of his tics may make them seem worse at first, because he is noticing tics that used to occur without his awareness. It is important to encourage the patient to hang in there, because, over time, awareness will help him to manage his tics more effectively.

If you feel that the patient is unable to detect his own tics at this point, it can be useful to do the patient's tics yourself and have the patient point them out in you before having him point out the tics in himself. To do this, use the procedures described in this section but perform the tics yourself while the patient points them out. Praise the patient when he accurately detects one of your tics, and prompt him to do so when he fails to identify a tic you have done. Such practice may make it easier for the patient to detect his tics. It may also be helpful to have the patient watch videotapes of himself having tics and make attempts to point out the tics on the recording.

Competing Response Training

The core of HRT is CR training. A CR is a behavior the patient can engage in when the urge to tic appears or soon after the tic has started. Research shows that the CR is an essential component of HRT (Woods et al., 1996) and that it must be implemented as soon as the tic or premonitory urge occurs (Miltenberger & Fuqua, 1985). However, it is not clear how the CR actually affects change in HRT. Two hypotheses exist. Some believe that HRT simply competes with the tic for prominence in the circuitry of the basal ganglia (the deep brain structures that help control movement). In other words, intentionally sending a signal to do the CR when a tic is about to happen prevents the basal ganglia from producing a tic. A second hypothesis is that the CR produces an effect because it makes the patient habituate to the premonitory urge. Because the actual mechanism behind the efficacy of the CR has remained untested, the CR should be done contingent on the tic or premonitory urge. *Anytime the competing response is done, it should be held for at least 1 min or until the premonitory urge fades away—whichever is longer.*

In this manual, the CR is implemented in three phases:

1. Selecting a CR

2. Demonstrating the CR and its correct implementation

3. Practicing the correct implementation of the CR

Selecting the Competing Response

CR training is done to teach the patient to engage in another behavior (called the competing response, or CR) for 1 min or until the urge to tic goes away (whichever is longer), contingent on the occurrence of the tic or a signal to tic. When selecting a behavior to be used as a CR, the following criteria should be used.

1. The behavior should either be physically incompatible with the target tic or should be a relaxed, more natural, graceful variation of the original tic, which may include trying to modify the tic so only part of the tic movement is expressed. Although both options may be effective, it is preferable to start with a physically incompatible behavior. A more subtle variation of a tic should be used only if the physically incompatible option has failed.

2. The CR should optimally be able to be maintained for at least 1 min or until the premonitory urge(s) goes away or is (are) significantly reduced.

3. The CR should be socially inconspicuous (or at least, less conspicuous than the tic) and easily compatible with normal ongoing activities.

4. Feedback from the patient as to what CR would work the best is crucial. Work with the patient in a collaborative fashion to select the CR.

Using these guidelines, it is clear that various CRs exist for the different topographies of tics. Although there is no "correct" CR, Table 4.1 lists common CRs for use with different motor tics.

Table 4.1 List of Possible Competing Responses for Different Motor Tics

Tic	Competing response
Body Jerk	Tighten stomach and buttocks muscles
Body twist	Stand or sit up straight while tensing back and keep hands to side (or in pockets, under legs)
Evening out	Hold arms at side
Eye blinking	Controlled, voluntary eye blinking
	Stare ahead, focus on object
Eyebrow movements (i.e., raise eyebrows or frowning)	Slow, controlled eye blink
	Stare at one point, end with one controlled eye blink
Eye close and hold	Controlled eye blink

continued

Table 4.1 List of Possible Competing Responses for Different Motor Tics *continued*

Tic	Competing response
Eye darting	Stay focused on one spot in the room and engage in smooth, controlled blinking
Eye widening	Tense eyebrows and use controlled breathing
Facial grimacing	Purse lips together gently
Nose scrunching	Pull nose down slightly, keep lips pressured shut, deep breathing
Finger movements (i.e., hair twirl, head rubbing)	Place hands on knees, squeezing if needed
	Cross arms
Flicking toes, curling toes	Press all toes flat on ground
Head nodding, head jerking	Tense neck muscles gently, fixate eyes
	Straighten and tense neck while lowering and tensing shoulders
Jaw clicking or thrusting	Let jaw hang loosely while doing relaxed breathing, holding breath for 2–3 s prior to exhale
	Close mouth and tense jaw
Knuckle cracking	Cross arms
	Fold hands
Leg lift or ankle twist	Push heels into floor
	Hold knees together tightly
Leg tensing	Tense buttocks
Licking Lips	Clench jaw softly, pressure lips together
Mouth opening	Purse lips, push teeth together, and push tongue up to roof of mouth
Neck roll	Tense neck muscles with chin down slightly
Nose twitching	Breathe in and out through mouth while tensing nose and eyebrows
	Purse lips and tense nose
Nostril flaring	Clench jaw and pressure lips together
Picking lips	Place hands on leg, squeezing if needed
Shaking head side-to-side	Tense neck in place, push chin toward chest and deep breathe
Shaking head up and down	Hold chin down to chest and deep breathe
	Tense neck muscles
Shoulder popping or shrugging	Push hand down on thigh and push elbow toward hip
	Tense shoulders in downward position, keep arms at sides
Spitting	Purse lips and use diaphragmatic breathing
Tensing arm or flailing arm	Interlock fingers, push shoulders down, and push arms into side
	If standing up, push arms into side and push shoulders down
Tongue clicking	Push tongue to roof of mouth, close mouth, and breathe
Wrist twisting	Hand on leg, squeeze leg if needed

For vocal tics, a "controlled" breathing CR should be implemented. Controlled breathing involves inhaling through the nose or mouth and exhaling through the nose or mouth. On the inhale, the patient's abdomen should expand, while her shoulders remain stationary. On the exhale, the patient's abdomen should contract, while her shoulders again remain stationary. When choosing a CR for a vocal tic, it is important to consider the inhalation/exhalation patterns (e.g., in/out through nose/mouth). The inhalation/exhalation pattern for the CR should always be the opposite of that used for completion of the tic. For example, if a patient exhibits a snorting tic that involves inhalation through the nose and exhalation through the mouth, the CR should involve diaphragmatic breathing where inhalation occurs through the mouth and exhalation through the nose.

Introduce the concept of the CR and ensure that the chosen CR will be acceptable to the patient. Forcing the patient to accept an unacceptable CR can lead to poor treatment compliance. The CR may be introduced as follows.

> *Now we're going to work on learning to manage your head-shaking tic. You're going to learn to do something we call a "competing response," although to make it easier, we'll just call them your "exercises." The purpose of these exercises is to give you something to help resist having to do your tic. After you do this long enough, your brain may learn that the tic doesn't need to occur, and the tic gets very weak or even goes away completely. For head shaking tics, the best exercise we've found is to hold your head in a certain way. I'll show you this exercise in a few minutes. You will need to do this head exercise for 1 min or until the urge goes away (whichever is longer) each time you have a head shaking tic or notice one of the tic signals we talked about earlier.*

(Demonstrate CR for patient as described in the next section.)

> *You've seen the exercise you'll be expected to do. Remember, you'll be asked to do this for 1 min or until the urge goes away each time you do the tic or notice a tic signal. To help you be comfortable with these exercises, we're going to practice them for a little while.*

After agreeing on a CR for the target tic, instruct the patient to record it on the Tics, Tic Signals, and Competing Responses form in the workbook. See the sample worksheet shown in Figure 4.1 for an example of how this could be done.

Teach the Patient to Do the Competing Response

Therapist Note

Keep in mind that it is ultimately more important that the patient practice the competing response rather than you simulating it for the patient. As such, you should feel free to shorten this section of the manual to facilitate adequate opportunity for the patient to practice the CR.

After choosing the CR, model the CR and its correct implementation for the patient. The patient will be expected to use the CR for 1 min or until the urge goes away, contingent on the occurrence of a tic or of one of the tic signals identified during awareness training. In modeling the CR to the patient, you could say something like the following:

Now I'd like to show you what your exercises will look like. I want you to tense your neck muscles slightly and tilt your chin down a bit. Hold this position for a minute or until the urge to tic goes away. I know these exercises may feel very strange at first because you are not used to holding your body like this, but the more you practice, the more normal it will seem.

When we use these exercises to treat your head shaking, I'm going to ask you to do them for 1 minute or until the urge goes away each time you do the tic or when you notice one of your tic signals we talked about earlier. As soon as you notice the tic or a signal, you need to do your exercises for 1 minute or until the urge goes away. Let me show you what I mean.

Engage in the tic and then implement the CR for 1 min. Remind the patient that at the end of 1 min, he should ask himself whether the urge is still present. If so, the CR should be continued. Next, demonstrate a warning sign for the tic followed by the CR for 1 min. This process should be continued until the patient has seen you use the CR for 1 min contingent on the tic and all of the patient's warning signs. While demonstrating the CR, it is important to keep conversing with patient. The patient needs to see that his life and social interactions shouldn't stop entirely when doing a CR. This should be pointed out to the patient. When this has been completed, the patient is ready to learn the CR and its correct implementation.

After you have shown the patient how to do the CR, have him practice it in front of you while you provide feedback. Do this until you are comfortable that the patient is doing the CR correctly.

When the patient is able to do the competing behavior, teach him to implement it contingent on occurrences of the tic or warning signs. Introduce this concept as follows.

> *Now that you've seen me do this and we've practiced the behavior, we're going to use it to treat your neck shaking. The two times you are to use these exercises are (1) as soon as you start doing a tic, and (2) as soon as you notice one of your tic signals. As soon as either one of these two things happen, you should stop and do your exercises for 1 minute or until the urge goes away—whichever is longer. Remember that while you are doing your exercise, you should still try to pay attention to what is happening around you. You don't want to stop your life just to do the exercises. Sometimes, you might have to stop doing other things to do the exercises, and that's OK, but most of the time we want you do to the exercises while you continue doing other things.*

Have the patient pretend to start a tic and then do the CR for 1 min. You can use a timer or clock to demonstrate to the patient how long 1 min is. Next, have the patient go through each of his warning signs and perform the CR for 1 min.

If the patient does the simulation correctly, be sure to offer praise. If you recognize that the patient is doing something incorrectly, provide feedback.

After the patient has done the CR correctly, have him use the CR after actual occurrences of the tic or warning signs as they occur in session. If the tic is occurring at a low rate, continued practice with the simulated tics may be useful. Make sure to keep praising the patient for correctly implementing the CR. When the patient fails to use the CR, prompt him to use it and/or demonstrate the correct implementation. Continue practicing until the patient can correctly implement the CR on four of five consecutive occurrences of the tic. Instruct the patient to use the CR in a contingent fashion at all times and in all situations from this point forward. Also emphasize to the patient that it may be very difficult to catch each and every tic at the beginning of treatment and that this is normal. However, the patient should be encouraged to do the best he can, and if he misses a tic, it's okay—he should just try to catch the next one. The following dialogue can be used for encouragement.

You've done a great job with your exercises. You seem to have gotten very good at this. From now on I want you to use your exercises in the way we talked about. If you're in session with me or if you're at work or school, or if you're with your friends, I need you to use your exercises the way we've practiced here. Throughout the rest of the session, I'll be checking to see if you're doing your exercises correctly. If you miss an opportunity to use them, I'll remind you, but I want you to try very hard to use them every time you tic.

Notes on Using the Competing Response

As you start to do HRT, you may encounter a number of potentially confusing or frustrating issues. We attempt to predict and clarify these issues in the following sections.

Patient Loss of Enthusiasm

Occasionally, as patients improve, they become less vigilant in doing the CRs for the tics that remain. To counter this, the patient should be reminded up front that HRT requires vigilance. He should be cautioned that improvement in the tic is often rapid, and that patients often become lax in the implementation of the competing response as tics decrease.

Patient Frustration

Patients may be frustrated by early efforts at HRT. Sometimes patients feel they are frequently doing the CR at first. Encourage them to stick with the treatment regimen throughout the course of therapy, and remind them (using the Inconvenience Review discussed in Session 2) of why they are doing the work.

Therapist Confusion Regarding Treatment of Complex Tics

There is often confusion about how to treat complex tics. Should the therapist break up the tic into component behaviors and develop a CR for each component? Generally, during awareness training we identify the component behaviors involved in the complex tic. However, when it comes time to doing the CR, we develop a CR only for the first component behavior of the complex tic. The patient is then taught to do the CR for this component contingent on the premonitory urge for the complex tic or on the occurrence of the first component. If we are unable to decrease the tic at this point and find that the patient always continues to engage in the latter components of the complex tic, we identify CRs for the other components. Essentially, the rule is to stop the tic as early in the sequence as possible.

Intense Premonitory Urges

In some cases, especially early in treatment, you may encounter a child whose premonitory urge is particularly intense and lasts well past the 1-min CR duration. If this seems to be occurring, it can be useful to sit with the patient while they do the CR and ask them for a SUDS rating every 30 seconds. Graph the SUDS data as they are collected. While sitting with the patient, engage in day-to-day conversation, but periodically check in to collect the SUDS rating. Wait until the patient gets down to a 0–2 level (on a 0–10 point scale) before stopping the exercise. Show the patient the graph and point out how the urge decreased even though the tic did not happen. Replicate this exercise in session a few times. Typically what happens is that the time needed to reach a SUDS rating of 0–2decreases with repeated exposure to the urge.

Social Support

After the patient has learned to do the CR exercises, a family member should be trained to assist the patient in the implementation of the CR. Social support involves three components: (1) finding a support person, (2) training the support person to praise or acknowledge the patient for correctly doing the exercises, and (3) training the support person to remind the patient to use the CR correctly. The amount of social support used in treatment depends on the age, developmental level, and preference of the patient. With adults and older adolescents, the social support person's level of involvement should be negotiated with the patient. Some adolescents may not want a support person involved in their treatment. This is okay initially. However, if the patient demonstrates poor compliance or response to treatment in subsequent sessions, the use of an external support person should be revisited.

Role of the Support Person

In most cases, the support person should be a parent. Discuss the idea of a support person in the first session so he is available for Session 2.

In most cases, the parent will have watched you work with the child to implement the CR. If he was out of the room when this material was covered, describe the basic idea of the intervention. In doing so, you may say something like:

> *Thanks for agreeing to help out (name of patient) and I with treatment for his tic. (Patient) and I have been working on noticing when he tics. We've also been working on doing exercises that help him stop the tic. This is what the exercises look like. Each time he has a tic or when he has an urge to tic, he's supposed to do these exercises for 1 min or until his urge to tic goes away.*

Ask the patient to demonstrate the CR for the support person. When this has been done, describe the responsibilities of the support person as follows:

> *The support person or "helper" has two main jobs. One is to let (patient) know when he's done a good job with the exercises and the other is to remind him to do the exercises when he forgets.*

Make a point of telling the parents that they are not to ask the child about tics specifically. Tics should not be the focus of parent–child interactions. The child should be neither rewarded nor punished based on tic occurrence or nonoccurrence. All prompting and praising is done to improve compliance with the CR.

Praising Correct Implementation

Tell the support person that it is important to acknowledge correct implementation of the CR by the patient. Instruct the support person as follows:

> When Bill does the exercises, you should let him know he's done a good job by saying something like "Nice job" or "Way to go," or by letting him know in a way that's comfortable for you and him.

Model for the support person by having the patient do his tic and begin the CR. Praise the patient for doing it correctly. After you have modeled the correct use of praise, ask the patient again to simulate a tic and CR. Ask the support person to give the patient positive feedback. Make sure to praise the support person for his efforts and offer corrective feedback if necessary.

Prompting the Child

Instruct the support person how to prompt the patient to use the CR when the patient forgets or does not use the CR correctly. This concept could be introduced as follows.

> Right now, Bill is supposed to start his exercise as soon as he starts doing a head shaking tic. However, it is likely he'll forget to do this from time to time. When this happens, your job is to help him remember. If you see Bill shake his head, but he does not do his exercises, then you need to remind him to do so.

Ask the patient to simulate a tic, but instruct him not to use the CR. When the patient does a tic that is not followed by the prescribed CR, model the behavior of prompting the patient to use the CR. Say something such as "Bill, I think you just had a tic. Don't forget to use your exercises."

After modeling this for the support person, ask him to practice prompting the patient to use his CR. Have the patient simulate a tic, but not do the CR. Praise the support person for his efforts and offer corrective feedback if necessary.

Notes on Using Social Support

When providing social support, it is important that parents understand the following guidelines. Social support delivered inappropriately can further flame distressed parent–child relationships or can be misconstrued as punishment for the tics.

1. It is important that reminders from the support person be delivered in a noncontentious and supportive manner. It is often helpful for the patient, therapist, and support person to jointly negotiate the manner in which reminders are to be delivered.

2. It is important not to turn the social support component into a parent–child struggle. Help the parent to step out of the struggle with their child about the tics. The parent's role in HRT is simply to be of help to the child. Help involves praising the correct implementation of the CR and prompting the patient to do the exercises when appropriate. The parent should understand that it is the child's responsibility to either do or not do the CR following a prompt. The parent should not get into a struggle with the child about doing the CR by cajoling or criticizing the child.

Chapter 5 *Session 1*

(Corresponds to chapters 1 and 2 of the workbook)

Materials Needed

▪ Tic Symptom Hierarchy Tracker

Outline

▪ Establish rapport with patient and family

▪ Review history of tic disorder and related problems

▪ Introduce treatment rationale

▪ Provide psychoeducation about TS

▪ Work with patient to create tic hierarchy

▪ Introduce concept of function-based interventions (see Chapter 3)

▪ Present and discuss the behavioral reward program

▪ Teach patient and family how to monitor tics

▪ Assign homework

Working With Adults

When using the manual with adults, the following modifications are necessary in Session 1.

Materials Needed

Tic Symptom Hierarchy Tracker

In-Session Activities

Unnoticed tics for adults: When a tic is observed in adult patients, the clinician immediately asks the patient about the severity and frequency of this particular tic. Then the clinician and patient jointly decide if and when the tic will be targeted in treatment.

No behavioral reward program or age-appropriately modified rewards.

Start discussing or identifying social support person in Session 1. Have the patient bring this person to the next session (when working with children, this is done in Session 2).

Rapport Building

The assessment described in Chapter 2 should be conducted before initiating treatment. Begin by welcoming patient and family to treatment. Briefly review social, developmental, and academic history of the patient.

History of Tic Disorder

Ascertain brief patient history and family knowledge of tic disorder. Review past mental health treatment history, especially for tic disorder but also attending to OCD and ADHD. Review impact of tic disorder on past and current functioning of patient.

Rationale for Comprehensive Behavioral Intervention for Tics

Explain the purpose of behavior therapy for tics. The following sample dialogue may be helpful:

We are going to do two things in therapy. First, we're going to figure out when things happen in your life that make your tics worse and then see if we can keep these things from happening or at least make them have less of an impact on your tics. Second, we are going to teach you how to manage your tics better so they don't bother you as much. Let's say you have a tic that makes you shake your head. This can be embarrassing or annoying and maybe even a bother to other people who are around you. So what we'll do is teach you to do something else that won't be as noticeable. For example, instead of shaking your head, you could tense your neck muscles slightly. If you can learn to do things that are less noticeable than your tics, this may make things a lot easier for you.

Psychoeducation About Tic Disorders

The goal of psychoeducation is to reduce blame, stigma, and negative feelings related to the patient's symptoms. Although psychoeducation is covered in this session, you should feel free to distribute any additional information that may be helpful. When starting the psychoeducation component, the following rationale should be given to the parents and the patient:

When children and their parents come to us for help for their tics we find it useful if we go over what we know about tic disorders and give families a chance to ask any questions. For the next few minutes, we're going to review some information about tic disorders. If you have any questions, please don't hesitate to ask.

Diagnostic Criteria for Tic Disorders

Explain that there are three different types of tic disorders: Tourette syndrome (TS; called Tourette's disorder in *DSM-IV-TR*), chronic tic disorder (CTD), and transient tic disorder (TTD). Review the *DSM-IV-TR* criteria for each (refer the family to the tables in Chapter 1 of the workbook). Because patients often have a catastrophic perception of a TS diagnosis, it can be helpful to point out the arbitrariness among the different tic disorders. Note that TS is not necessarily a much more problematic condition.

Review the list of tics from Chapter 1 and have the patient and the family follow along using the List of Simple and Complex Tics (Table 1.4) in Chapter 1 of the workbook. Note that not everything a child does is a tic and sometimes it can be difficult to tell them apart. You may want to use the following dialogue:

> *You can see from these criteria that motor and vocal tics are the main symptoms of tic disorders. On the list in your workbook, you can see that there are a number of different types of tics including simple tics* (give examples) *and complex tics* (give examples). *One type of complex vocal tic that many people associate with tic disorders is coprolalia, or swearing tics. Although the popular media likes to make this seem like a common symptom, it actually doesn't happen for most people with tic disorders.*
>
> *As you probably noticed, tics don't occur in a steady way. Rather, they wax (get worse) and wane (get better) over the course of time.*

Phenomenology

People with tic disorders not only have the tics themselves, but they often have what are called "premonitory urges." These urges usually occur right before the tic. They feel similar to an urge to sneeze or scratch an itch. They are sometimes described as an "inner tension." Urges usually go away or get less intense for a little while right after a tic. Not all tics have urges associated with them, and younger patients are less likely to have them than older patients.

Table 5.1 lists areas of the body where urges are commonly felt. Refer patient or parents to the same table in Chapter 1 of the workbook.

People with tic disorders also sometimes are very sensitive to things going on around them. They may be bothered by particular sensory stimuli such as tags in clothing or textures of fabrics. Also, certain words or sounds may trigger tics. Some patients have urges to do dangerous or forbidden acts such as shouting in church or opening the door of a moving car. Other patients have what we call "just right" behavior, which is when the patient has to do something in a certain way until it is arranged properly or "evened up," or until it feels "just

Table 5.1 Common Areas for Premonitory Urges

Left palm
Right shoulder blade
Right palm
Left shoulder
Left shoulder blade
Midline abdomen
Throat
Right shoulder
Back of right hand
Front of right thigh
Front of right foot
Back of left hand
Inside of right upper arm
Front of left thigh
Left eye
Right eye

Note. Adapted from Leckman, Walker, and Cohen (1993).

right." Sometimes these latter behaviors can be construed as symptoms of OCD. Refer to Chapter 2 for a discussion of the distinction between tic symptoms and OCD symptoms.

Natural History of Tics

Tics usually start around the age of 5–7 and usually increase in frequency and intensity up to around the age of 10–11 (refer to Tables 5.2 and 5.3 and the corresponding tables in Chapter 1 of the workbook). Tic disorders are more common in boys, and the severity of symptoms tends to decrease in adulthood.

Social Difficulties and Comorbidities

Some patients with tic disorders experience social and academic difficulties, but these problems may be caused by other disorders that go

Table 5.2 Age-of-Onset-Distribution for Tics

Age	Number of cases out of 221
1	4
2	7
3	22
4	22
5	32
6	28
7	24
8	21
9	22
10	15
11	7
12	6
13	4
14	2
15	3
16	2

Note. Adapted from Leckman, King, and Cohen (1999).

Table 5.3 Percentage of Clients Stating the Age of Worst Ever Tic Severity

Age	% of clients
1	0
2	0
3	0
4	0
5	0
6	5
7	7
8	7
9	18
10	16
11	11

Age	% of clients
12	18
13	14
14	5
15	0
16	2
17	0
18	0

Note. Adapted from Bloch et al. (2006).

along with tic disorders and not the tics themselves. In other words, if a patient has a tic disorder only, she is at a lower risk of experiencing social and academic difficulties when compared to those who also have ADHD, for example. In TS clinics, approximately 50% of people with TS have ADHD, and about 30% have OCD in addition to their tics.

Introduction to Causes

Begin by saying that you will be discussing the causes of tic disorder. The following dialogue may be helpful in your introduction to the topic:

I am sure you know other kids in your class with asthma or diabetes. Having tics is similar to that . . . you will always have your tics, just like asthma, but with medication, talking to people about it, and seeing doctors occasionally, you can learn to control it so that it doesn't get in the way of you living your life and doing things you want to do.

Just like asthma or diabetes, tics are a medical illness with a genetic basis and are greatly affected by our lifestyle and what happens in our lives. Today we're going to spend a few minutes talking about the causes of tics.

Genetics

Explain that although there is an inherited component to tic disorders, it is unlikely that one gene is responsible. It appears that a certain genetic makeup involving many genes puts patients at a greater risk of developing tic disorders.

Neurological Basis

Evidence suggests that specific circuits in the brain are responsible for many symptoms of tic disorders. These circuits are known as the cortico-striatal-thalamo-cortical (CSTC) circuits. Explain to the patient or parents using the following sample dialogue:

> *In all brains, signals from the cortex, or the part of the brain that* ***plans*** *movements, get sent to the part of the brain that* ***controls*** *movements and then loops back into the front part of the brain. In patients with tic disorders, it may be that the part of the brain that inhibits movement is not working properly.*

Explain that in addition to these brain structures, the chemical systems within these structures play a role in tic expression. For example, high levels of dopamine activity have been implicated in tics. Other neurotransmitters that may be involved in tics include glutamate, GABA, serotonin, and norepinephrine. Medications used to treat tics may alter these chemical systems. Although there isn't direct evidence that the procedure described in this workbook actually affects brain chemistry, we do know that learning can produce changes in the way the brain works.

Other Risk or Protective Factors

Other events have also been found to worsen tics or put someone at greater risk of developing a tic disorder. For example, factors that influence the development and function of certain brain circuits include premature birth, maternal stress during pregnancy, prolonged labor, fetal distress, and use of forceps. It may also be the case that some patients develop tics in reaction to recurrent strep infections. It is important to note that although these factors may be related to tics, they do not necessarily cause tics.

Prevalence

Finally, discuss the prevalence of Tourette syndrome and CTDs. You may use the following sample dialogue:

> *One last thing I wanted to discuss with you is how many people actually have tics. The best available evidence from the most recent studies indicates that 3–8 school-age children per 1000 have TS. The prevalence of CTDs or TTDs is less certain—but altogether, the prevalence of tic disorders may be as high as 4% in children. From these numbers, you can tell that tic disorders are not "rare" in school-age children. Given what we know about the natural history of TS, the prevalence of TS and tic disorders are likely to be lower in adulthood.*

At this point, ask the patient and/or parents whether they have any questions.

Normalize the disorder and reduce stigma and anxiety about "being crazy." Stress that while tic disorders can run in families, neither the patient nor their parents caused it. Recommend bibliotherapy (e.g., "What Makes Ryan Tick"; Hughes, 1996) to show that others kids have the same problem and that they are not alone, or "crazy." Note the list of resources provided in the appendix at the end of this book. The same appendix appears in the corresponding workbook as well.

Creating a Tic Hierarchy

Using the Tic Symptom Hierarchy Tracker in Chapter 2 of the workbook, help the patient develop a comprehensive list of her current tics. The symptom checklist portion of the Yale Global Tic Severity Scale (YGTSS) can be used to facilitate this procedure. A parent(s) can also aid in listing the tics. All current tics noted by the parents and the patient should be listed.

After the tics have been identified, work with the patient to create operational definitions for each tic she currently exhibits. For example, if the patient has a neck shaking tic, you may agree on the following definition, "A neck shaking tic is when your head departs from midline, moves left, and then returns to midline." Obtaining operational definitions for all current tics allows you to communicate effectively with the patient and allows you to accurately count tics during assessment.

After the tics have been identified and operationally defined, ask the patient to rate how bothersome each tic is on a scale of 0–10 and record the Subjective Units of Discomfort (SUDS) rating on the Tic Symptom Hierarchy Tracker. A rating of 0 indicates that a tic either is not occurring or produces absolutely no distress/discomfort. A score of 10 indicates that the tic is creating significant amounts of distress or discomfort. See the sample, completed hierarchy shown in Figure 5.1. This completed form shows a child with five tics.

Treatment is based on the tics identified in this hierarchy. Generally, we start with the most bothersome tic that the clinician, patient, and her parents or significant others feel is most likely to meet with success. For example, our clinical experience suggests that tics involving the eyes (e.g., eye rolling and eye blinking) are more difficult to treat, so if these are rated as most troubling, we typically start with a different tic. Addressing an easier-to-treat tic first will allow the patient to meet with early success that may facilitate motivation in later therapy sessions.

If you notice a tic in session that the patient and parents do not note, then you should gently state that you noticed the tic and ask the patient

Symptom			SUDS Rating		
Session #:	1	2	3	4
Date:	12/1	12/8	12/15	12/22
1. Arm jerking: pull arm back when it's bent at elbow	2	3	2	3
2. Head shaking: moving head rapidly to the right	7	6	5	5
3. Coughing: short hard cough	8	9	9	3
4. Leg/head tic: rapidly bring legs together and then stretch neck	9	10	6	5
5. Blink	2	3	2	2

Figure 5.1

Example of a Completed Tic Symptom Hierarchy Tracker

or parents whether they have ever noticed it themselves. Tics noted only by you should not be put on the hierarchy immediately, but in subsequent weeks you should again bring up the tic and ask whether the patient or parents would like to rate the severity of that tic and put it on the hierarchy.

Sometimes confusion is created by determining whether a complex tic should be listed as one tic, or as a series of individual tics. Our general rule is that if any component of a complex tic occurs separately from the complex tic, then it should be listed as its own tic in addition to being included in the description of the complex tic. If components of the complex tic do not occur separately, we recommend that the complex tic be defined as a single tic with multiple components.

Introduce Concept of Function-Based Intervention

Review the material in Chapter 3. Introduce the concept of function-based interventions to the parents and child by describing the rationale and how the factors that influence tics for that child are determined. Discuss also how interventions are chosen. Beginning in Session 2, each tic being addressed in HRT will also be functionally assessed and a function-based treatment implemented.

Rationale

Point out to the parent that research clearly shows that various factors in the child's life can make tics better or worse. These factors can come before tics occur or right after, and they can affect children in different ways.

Discuss with the parent that even though some of the interventions can make it seem like the child has been doing the tics intentionally, this is not the case. Even though getting out of activities or receiving attention for tics can make them happen more, tics are not intentional things children do to avoid certain activities or to get attention.

Events That Affect Tics

Explain to the parents that you will use two methods for determining what events affect their child's tics. First, in each session, a functional assessment interview will be conducted for the tic being addressed in that session. This will involve you, the patient, and parents discussing different events that may make tics more likely to happen (see Chapter 3). Explain to the parents that it will be important to provide as much detail about those situations as possible.

Second, the patient and the parents will be given homework assignments, starting today, to observe the tics at home. Using the Functional Assessment Self-Report Form in the workbook, the patient or the parents will record occurrences of tics, including when and in what situations they seem to be worse. Such information will be helpful in developing the treatments specifically for the patient.

Behavioral Reward Program

The purpose of the behavioral reward system is to motivate the patient to attend sessions, participate in session activities, complete homework assignments, and increase general compliance with therapy. One of the primary reasons behavior therapy fails to produce behavior change involves poor treatment compliance (Carr, Bailey, Carr, & Coggin, 1996). Thus, the focus is on rewarding compliance and attendance. It is important to note that the behavioral reward program is not designed to reward tic reduction, only efforts in management.

Rationale

The first step in any behavioral reward system is to provide a rationale. The parents and the patient should be reassured that you understand that therapy is hard work and that the patient should be rewarded for doing this work. To do so, you, the patient, and the parents are going to work together to decide upon a fair and feasible reward system. The following rationale should be given to the parents and the patient.

Coming to session and doing the homework assignments is hard work,
so we'd like to come up with a system to reward (patient) for his/her
hard work. For the next few minutes we are going to come up with a
few things or activities that (patient) can earn for coming to sessions,
doing homework, and working hard in session. These rewards are
given for trying hard, not for reducing tics. Although we hope the tics
will get better, we're really interested in having (patient) work hard
and give treatment his/her best shot.

Explain that the reinforcement program involves the delivery of points
or stickers contingent on specific behaviors. These include attending
sessions, attempting or completing in-session tasks, and completing
homework assignments. When explaining the program, emphasize that
points are given for doing these behaviors, but not for reporting reductions in tic occurrence. Points or stickers are exchangeable for tangible
rewards which will be predetermined by the patient and the therapist
at an exchange rate also negotiated by the therapist between the patient
and the parents.

After explaining the aforementioned rationale and general layout of the
reinforcement program, you should negotiate the tangible rewards that
can be earned for the specified behaviors and set the exchange rate.

Identify Rewards

Identify several small and inexpensive items and/or activities that the
patient finds rewarding. Allow the patient to respond first, but follow-
up with the parents to identify activities and items that the parents have
found useful in the past. After several items and activities have been
identified, have the patient rank them in order of most to least rewarding. Next, ask the parents to remove any items/activities that are not
feasible (i.e., too expensive, difficult to obtain, forbidden, etc.)

Therapist Note

▨ *We recommend providing these rewards yourself, so don't agree to*
anything that you cannot provide. ▨

Set Exchange

Next, inform the patient what she must do to obtain the reward. The exchange should be decided upon by you and is nonnegotiable once established. For example, the patient may get one point for attending each session, one point for doing all homework assigned in previous sessions, and one point for participating in the previous session. When the patient earns the predetermined number of points (e.g., 21 of 24 possible points), then she receives the chosen reward.

Review Date

Establish a time during the session in which performance will be evaluated for reinforcer exchange. For example, at the end of a session, you can tell the patient and the parents that the patient earned a reward for attending the day's session and another reward for making an effort during the session. Likewise, if the patient complied with the homework during the prior week, the patient could earn the reward attached to homework compliance, which could be noted during the session. Each week, the behavioral reward program is revisited and points earned are recorded and progress toward the final goal praised. When the plan is complete, have the patient fill out the Behavioral Reward Form in the workbook. See Figure 5.2 for a sample, completed Behavioral Reward Form.

Self-Monitoring Training

Direct the family to the tic self-monitoring forms provided in the workbook. Have the parents use the Tic Monitoring Sheet for Parents to monitor the first tic, chosen in this session, a minimum of 3–4 times over the next week. Both the patient and the parents will be involved in keeping tally marks that record each occurrence of the first tic during an agreed-upon time interval (15–30 min). Ask patient and parents to choose a period of time for monitoring tics (e.g., when patient is sitting down watching TV or doing homework) when parents will be

Child: _Billy_

Session # _3_   Date of Session _5/1/2008_

Establish Reward

Determine the reward for each target behavior. If points toward a larger reward are used, note how many points for each behavior are earned each time behavior occurs.

Target Behavior #1 (Attending Session)

Reward: _1 point_

Target Behavior #2 (Completing Homework)

Reward: _1 point_

Target Behavior #3 (In Session Activity)

Reward: _1 point_

Target Behavior # 4 (Other: _____)

Reward: _____

Exchange

Determine how many points will be needed to acquire a larger reward and note which reward will be earned.

21 points can be exchanged for a $15 gift card to a bookstore

Review Date

Determine when points will be awarded and the totals reviewed.

At the end of each session, we will see how many points have been earned and review how many have been earned toward achieving the goal.

Figure 5.2

Example of Behavioral Reward Program

available to monitor the patient carefully. Choose a time period when tic occurrence is likely.

In addition to these structured monitoring times, encourage the patient to use the My Tic Sheet to self-monitor the first tic on the hierarchy whenever she can (e.g., when alone, at school, and around bedtime) and do something unnoticeable to others like saying "T" under her breath each time the tic occurs.

Homework

✎ Have the patient monitor the first tic on the hierarchy using the My Tic Sheet in the workbook.

✎ Have parents monitor the first tic on the hierarchy using the Tic Monitoring Sheet for Parents in the workbook.

✎ Have the child (with or without parent assistance) complete the Functional Assessment Self-Report Form in the workbook. Review instructions for completion with the patient or the parents.

Chapter 6   *Session 2*

(Corresponds to chapter 3 of the workbook)

Materials Needed

- Tic Symptom Hierarchy Tracker (completed in Session 1)

- Functional Assessment Form (FAF)

- List of sample function-based interventions from Chapter 3

- List of competing responses (CRs) from Chapter 4

Outline

- Review events of the past week and update tic hierarchy

- Review homework and reward program

- Conduct inconvenience review

- Conduct functional assessment and present related treatment strategies for first tic on hierarchy

- Conduct HRT for Tic 1

- Assign homework

Working With Adults

When using the manual with adults, the following modifications are necessary in Session 2.

Materials Needed

FAF—Adult Version

In-Session Activities

When reviewing events of the past week (see following section) ask adult patients about the impact of tic symptoms on work, social, and family functioning

No behavioral reward program or age-appropriately modified reward

Weekly and Hierarchy Review

Review the events of the past week. Query the patient and the parents about:

Any significant events in the patient's life

Tic symptoms and impact on school, social, and family functioning

At least one positive event or thing from patient that occurred since last session

Review the patient's Tic Symptom Hierarchy Tracker and have him provide SUDS ratings for the past week. Revise the hierarchy as needed, considering that old tics may resolve and new ones may appear.

Homework and Behavioral Reward Program Review

Reward any compliance with monitoring homework. Review any new information stemming from the Functional Assessment Self-Report Form completed in Session 1.

Reframe noncompliance to reduce negative feelings in the patient, problem-solve compliance difficulties, and encourage the patient to comply with homework over the coming week. At the time agreed upon in Session 1, assign points for any behavior covered in the behavioral reward program (i.e., points for attendance, doing homework, and participating in the prior session).

Inconvenience Review

Help the patient create a list of things that he dislikes about his tics. For example, explain that other kids list such things as, "It's embarrassing, and people tease me," or "I don't like explaining it to new people I meet," or "It gets in the way when I write, play sports, etc." Have the patient develop his own list of reasons why his tics are inconvenient, embarrassing, distressing, and annoying. Use this list as a motivator the patient can keep in mind to help him do the treatment.

Have the patient record this list on the Tic Hassles Form in the workbook. As his management of the tics improves, the patient can cross items off the list as they no longer are relevant. Review this list at each session.

Function-Based Assessment and Interventions for First Tic

- Remind the patient and the parents of the purposes of the function-based intervention.

- Conduct the functional assessment interview described in Chapter 3.

- Review the functional-assessment self-report data assigned at the end of Session 1.

- Use these data to work with the patient and the parents to develop function-based interventions using the five principles described in Chapter 3. Remind the parents and patient of the five principles of function-based interventions.

- On the Function-Based Interventions Form in the patient's workbook, write down the agreed-upon interventions and work with the parents to determine a concrete plan for how these interventions will be implemented in the child's life.

Habit Reversal Training for First Tic

Review the material in Chapter 4, paying particular attention to the section on social support. The child's support person will be identified and trained during this session.

Implement HRT for the first tic using the procedures outlined in this section. This tic should be the same tic as targeted in the function-based interventions earlier in the session. As you target the tic remember to do the following procedures.

Introduce awareness training

Define the tic

Describe antecedent sensations and behaviors

Acknowledge tics and tic signals

Select the CR

Teach the patient to do the CR

Identify the support person and describe the purpose of social support

Teach support person to praise the patient for doing HRT correctly

Teach support person to prompt patient to do HRT when necessary

Homework

 Instruct the patient to use the CR developed for Tic 1 during both planned and unplanned times. Remind the parents to use the social support component.

✎ Have the family do planned CR practice at least 3–4 times this week, for at least 30 min each time. During the planned exercises, both patient and parent(s) should monitor the tic using the My Tic Sheet and Tic Monitoring Sheet for Parents in the workbook (refer Session 1 for monitoring procedures).

✎ Have the parents remind the child of the reward system to encourage compliance and boost motivation.

✎ Have parents implement the interventions on the Function-Based Interventions Form in the workbook.

Chapter 7   *Session 3*

(Corresponds to chapter 4 of the workbook)

Materials Needed

- Tic Symptom Hierarchy Tracker Form

- Functional Assessment Form (FAF)

- List of sample function-based interventions from Chapter 3

- List of competing responses (CRs) from Chapter 4

Outline

- Review events of the past week and update tic hierarchy

- Review homework and reward efforts

- Conduct inconvenience review

- Review treatment procedures for Tic 1

- Conduct functional assessment and present related treatment strategies for next tic on hierarchy

- Conduct HRT for next tic

- Assign homework

Working With Adults

When using the manual with adults, the following modifications are necessary in Session 3.

Materials Needed

FAF—Adult Version

In-Session Activities

When reviewing events of the past week (see following section), ask adult patients about the impact of tic symptoms on work, social, and family functioning

No behavioral reward program or age-appropriately modified reward

Weekly and Hierarchy Review

Review the events of the past week. Query the patient and parents about:

Any significant events in the patient's life

Tic symptoms and impact on school, social, and family functioning

At least one positive event or thing from patient that occurred since last session

Note any situations in which tics were increased and explore factors that may have contributed to the exacerbation

Review the Tic Symptom Hierarchy Tracker and have the patient provide SUDS ratings for the past week. Revise the list as needed, considering that old tics may resolve and new ones may appear.

Homework Review

Reward any compliance with monitoring homework. Reframe non-compliance to reduce negative feelings in the patient, problem-solve compliance difficulties, and encourage the patient to comply with homework over the coming week. At the time agreed upon in Session 1, assign points for any behavior covered in the behavioral reward program (i.e., points for attending, doing homework, and participating in the prior session).

Inconvenience Review

Review with the patient the Tic Hassles Form completed in Session 2. Use this review to attempt to sustain the patient's motivation to work on tics.

Review Function-Based Intervention and Competing Response for Tic 1

Discuss any difficulties with function-based intervention protocol for Tic 1, and problem-solve these in session. Modify function-based intervention as needed given feedback from the past week to maximize ease of administration and compliance.

Review CR for first tic and have the patient practice implementing it. Discuss any difficulties with CR implementation and problem-solve these in session. Modify CR as needed given patient feedback from the past week to maximize ease of administration and compliance.

Function-Based Assessment and Interventions for Next Tic

- Remind the patient and the parents of the purposes of the function-based intervention.

- Conduct the functional assessment interview described in Chapter 3 for the next tic on the hierarchy.

- Review the functional assessment self-report data assigned at the end of Session 1.

- Use these data to work with the patient and the parents to develop function-based interventions using the five principles described in Chapter 3. Remind the parents and the patient of the five principles of function-based interventions.

On the Function-Based Interventions Form, write down the agreed-upon interventions and work with the parents to determine a concrete plan for how these interventions will be implemented in the child's life.

Habit Reversal Training for Next Tic

Review the material in Chapter 4. Implement HRT for the next tic using the procedures outlined in this section. This tic should be the same tic as targeted in the function-based interventions from earlier in the session. As you target the tic remember to do the following procedures.

Introduce awareness training

Define the tic

Describe antecedent sensations and behaviors

Acknowledge tics and tic signals

Select the CR

Teach the patient to do the CR

Teach the support person to praise the patient for doing HRT correctly

Teach the support person to prompt the patient to do HRT when necessary

Homework

✎ Instruct the patient to use the CRs for Tics 1 and 2 during both planned and unplanned times. Refer to the Tics, Tic Signals, and Competing Responses form. Remind parents to use social support for both tics.

✎ Have the family do planned CR practice at least 3–4 times for both Tics 1 and 2, for at least 30 min each time. During the planned

exercises, both patient and parent(s) should monitor the tic using the
My Tic Sheet and Tic Monitoring Sheet for Parents in the workbook
(refer to Session 1 for monitoring procedures).

✎ Have parents remind the child of the reward system to encourage
compliance and boost motivation.

✎ Have parents implement the interventions on the Function-Based
Interventions Form in the workbook.

Chapter 8   *Session 4*

(Corresponds to chapters 4 and 5 of the workbook)

Materials Needed

- Tic Symptom Hierarchy Tracker Form
- Functional Assessment Form (FAF)
- List of sample function-based interventions from Chapter 3
- List of competing responses (CRs) from Chapter 4

Outline

- Review events of the past week and update tic hierarchy
- Review homework and reward efforts.
- Conduct inconvenience review
- Review treatment procedures for Tics 1 and 2
- Conduct functional assessment and present related treatment strategies for next tic on hierarchy
- Conduct HRT for next tic
- Introduce relaxation training
- Conduct diaphragmatic breathing exercise
- Assign homework

Working With Adults

When using the manual with adults, the following modifications are necessary in Session 4.

Materials Needed

FAF—Adult Version

In-Session Activities

When reviewing events of the past week (see following section) ask adult patients about the impact of tic symptoms on work, social, and family functioning.

No behavioral reward program or age-appropriately modified reward.

Weekly and Hierarchy Review

Review the events of the past week. Query the patient and parents about:

Any significant events in the patient's life

Tic symptoms and impact on school, social, and family functioning

At least one positive event or thing from patient that occurred since last session

Note any situations in which tics were increased and explore factors that may have contributed to the exacerbation

Review the Tic Symptom Hierarchy Tracker and have the patient provide SUDS ratings for the past week. Revise the list as needed, considering that old tics may resolve and new ones may appear.

Homework Review

Reward any compliance with monitoring homework. Reframe non-compliance to reduce negative feelings in the patient, problem-solve compliance difficulties, and encourage the patient to comply with homework over the coming week. At the time agreed on in Session 1, assign points for any behavior covered in the behavioral reward program (i.e., points for attending, doing homework, and participating in the prior session).

Inconvenience Review

Review with the patient the Tic Hassles Form completed in Session 2. Use this review to attempt to sustain the patient's motivation to work on tics.

Review Function-Based Interventions and Competing Responses for Tics 1 and 2

Discuss any difficulties with function-based intervention protocols for Tics 1 and 2, and problem-solve these in session. Modify function-based intervention as needed given feedback from the past week to maximize ease of administration and compliance.

Review CR implementation for the Tics 1 and 2, and problem-solve these in session. Modify CR as needed given patient feedback from the past week to maximize ease of administration and compliance.

Function-Based Assessment and Interventions for Next Tic

- Remind the patient and the parents of the purposes of the function-based intervention.

- Conduct the functional assessment interview described in Chapter 3 for the next tic on the hierarchy.

- Review the functional assessment self-report data assigned at the end of Session 1.

- Use these data to work with the patient and the parents to develop function-based interventions using the five principles described in Chapter 3. Remind the parents and the patient of the five principles of function-based interventions.

On the Function-Based Interventions Form, write down the agreed-upon interventions and work with the parents to determine a concrete plan for how these interventions will be implemented in the child's life.

Habit Reversal Training for Next Tic

Review the material in Chapter 4. Implement HRT for the next tic using the procedures outlined in this section. This tic should be the same tic as targeted in the function-based interventions from earlier in the session. As you target the tic, remember to do the following procedures.

Introduce awareness training

Define the tic

Describe antecedent sensations and behaviors

Acknowledge tics and tic signals

Select the CR

Teach the patient to do the CR

Teach the support person to praise the patient for doing HRT correctly

Teach the support person to prompt the patient to do HRT when necessary

Introduction of Relaxation Techniques

At this point in the session, you will introduce the patient to relaxation. Provide the following rationale:

Now we are going to talk about something a little bit different, we are going to talk about how to relax. The reason it is important to learn how to relax is because tics make our muscles tense and leave our whole body tight and tense. This sometimes makes us feel upset or tired. For some kids, tics get worse when they have stress, when they are upset, or when their bodies are tired. Helping you to learn to relax might help your tics get better. Do you have any questions?

Answer any questions the patient may have. Describe that learning to relax will involve two skills: relaxed breathing and muscle relaxation. In this session start with breathing. You will train the patient in muscle relaxation in Session 5. Refer patient and/or parents to the Breathing Exercise Sheet in Chapter 5 of the workbook. Explain that throughout the relaxation exercise, you will ask the patient to rate how tense he is using a scale from 0 to 10, where 0 represents he is not tensed at all and 10 represents he is the most tensed.

Diaphragmatic Breathing Exercise

Tell the patient that today he is going to work on doing a type of relaxation called relaxed or diaphragmatic breathing. Use the following instructions:

When you breathe in, your stomach should go out, and when you breathe out, it should go back in. Breathe in through your nose and out through your mouth.

If the patient has difficulty with these instructions, use the following metaphor to illustrate:

Imagine that you are lying on your back and I put a balloon on your stomach. The game is—you have to try to make the balloon go up and down without using your arms. You can only use your stomach. One way to make your stomach move is to breathe in and out. Watch me (place hand on stomach). *When I breathe in, my stomach goes out, so the balloon will go up and down.*

After the patient is doing the breathing properly, have him practice the technique 5 times for 30 seconds each time.

After the exercise, discuss with the patient possible targeted times in which relaxed breathing may be useful in reducing stress. Identify two situations in the next week in which the patient can practice using relaxed breathing. Have the patient and/or parents write these situations down on the Breathing Exercise Sheet in the workbook.

Homewor k

✎ Instruct the patient to use the CRs for Tics 1–3 during both planned and unplanned times. Refer to the Tics, Tic Signals, and Competing Responses form. Remind parents to use social support for both tics.

✎ Have the family do planned CR practice at least 3–4 times for Tics 1–3, with special attention to the new tic, for at least 30 min each time. During the planned exercises, both patient and parent(s) should monitor the tic using the My Tic Sheet and Tic Monitoring Sheet for Parents in the workbook (refer to Session 1 for monitoring procedures).

✎ Have parents remind the child of the reward system to encourage compliance and boost motivation.

✎ Have parents implement the interventions on the Function-Based Interventions Form in the workbook.

✎ Ask the patient to practice relaxed breathing 5 min per day, 3–4 times per week, and to try using the breathing exercise in the identified tic-stressing situations.

Chapter 9   *Session 5*

(Corresponds to chapters 4 and 5 of the workbook)

Materials Needed

- Tic Symptom Hierarchy Tracker Form
- Functional Assessment Form (FAF)
- List of sample function-based interventions from Chapter 3
- List of competing responses (CRs) from Chapter 4

Outline

- Review events of the past week and update tic hierarchy
- Review homework and reward efforts
- Conduct inconvenience review
- Review treatment procedures for prior tics
- Conduct functional assessment and present related treatment strategies for next tic on hierarchy
- Conduct HRT for next tic
- Introduce progressive muscle relaxation (PMR)
- Conduct PMR exercise
- Assign homework

Working With Adults

When using the manual with adults, the following modifications are necessary in Session 5.

Materials Needed

FAF—Adult Version

In-Session Activities

When reviewing events of the past week (see following section), ask adult patients about the impact of tic symptoms on work, social, and family functioning

No behavioral reward program or age-appropriately modified reward

Weekly and Hierarchy Review

Review the events of the past week. Query the patient and parents about:

Any significant events in the patient's life

Tic symptoms and impact on school, social, and family functioning

At least one positive event or thing from patient that occurred since last session

Note any situations in which tics were increased and explore factors that may have contributed to the exacerbation

Review the patient's completed Tic Symptom Hierarchy Tracker and have the patient provide SUDS ratings for the past week. Revise the list as needed, considering that old tics may resolve and new ones may appear.

Homework Review

Reward any compliance with monitoring homework. Reframe non-compliance to reduce negative feelings in the patient, problem-solve compliance difficulties, and encourage the patient to comply with homework over the coming week. At the time agreed upon in Session 1, assign points for any behavior covered in the behavioral reward program (i.e., points for attending, doing homework, and participating in the prior session).

Inconvenience Review

Review with the patient the Tic Hassles Form completed in Session 2. Use this review to attempt to sustain the patient's motivation to work on tics.

Review Function-Based Interventions and Competing Responses for Tics 1–3

Review function-based intervention and practice CRs for previous tics. Discuss any difficulties with function-based intervention protocols for Tics 1–3, and problem-solve these in session. Modify function-based intervention as needed given feedback from the past week to maximize ease of administration and compliance.

Review CR implementation for the Tics 1–3 and problem-solve these in session. Modify CR as needed given patient feedback from the past week to maximize ease of administration and compliance.

Function-Based Assessment and Interventions for Next Tic

- Remind the patient and the parents of the purposes of the function-based intervention.

- Conduct the functional assessment interview described in Chapter 3 for the next tic on the hierarchy.

Review the functional assessment self-report data assigned at the end of Session 1.

Use these data to work with the patient and the parents to develop function-based interventions using the five principles described in Chapter 3. Remind the parents and the patient of the five principles of function-based interventions.

On the Function-Based Interventions Form, write down the agreed-upon interventions and work with the parents to determine a concrete plan for how these interventions will be implemented in the child's life.

Habit Reversal Training for Next Tic

Review the material in Chapter 4. Implement HRT for the next tic using the procedures outlined in this section. This tic should be the same tic as targeted in the function-based interventions from earlier in this session. As you target the tic remember to do the following procedures.

Introduce awareness training

Define the tic

Describe antecedent sensations and behaviors

Acknowledge tics and tic signals

Select the CR

Teach the patient to do the CR

Teach the support person to praise the patient for doing HRT correctly

Teach the support person to prompt the patient to do HRT when necessary

Before introducing the next relaxation exercise, review the relaxed breathing exercise practiced in the last session. Remind the patient of why she is learning to relax and that relaxation involves two parts: deep breathing and PMR. Then describe PMR. Start by going over all of the muscle groups to be used to make sure they can be tensed. The four muscle groups are:

1. arms and hands

2. legs, buttocks, and feet

3. chest and stomach

4. face, neck, and shoulders

Introduce the PMR exercise as follows:

> *The first thing we are going to do is to practice making our muscles tight. Do you know how to make your muscles tight? Good, lets practice. First, tighten your* _____. (Have the patient practice tightening each of the four muscle groups)

If the patient has difficulty knowing how to tense any of the muscle groups, try using the following dialogues:

Arms and Hands

> *The best way we've found to make your arms and hand tight is to make a fist with both hands and hold your elbows in really tight to your side like you're trying to squeeze yourself. Can you do this?*

Legs, Buttocks, and Feet

> *To tense these muscles, stick your legs out straight, lift them off the chair a little bit, and try to point your toes at your face.*

Chest and Stomach

Sometimes muscles are hard to tense, so let's try this exercise. Imagine that you are lying on the ground and a giant purple elephant is going to step on your stomach and you need to make your stomach hard until the elephant goes by. Can you make your stomach hard?

Face, Neck, and Shoulders

To tense your face, neck, and shoulders bring your shoulders up toward your ears, put your chin down and make it try to touch your chest. While you're doing this, clench your teeth a little bit, pull back your mouth like you're screaming, and open your eyes wide.

PMR Exercise

Once the patient understands how to tighten the muscles, have her tense (5–7 seconds) and relax (20 seconds) each muscle group twice. After each step, remind the patient to breathe correctly (diaphragmatic or relaxed breathing) as described in Session 4. You may use the following script:

OK, now I would like for you to think about the muscles in your
_____. I would like you to tense the muscles in
the _____ now. Hold and feel how
tight/heavy/warm/tense it's getting (pause 5–7 seconds). And, relax
(pause 20 seconds).

OK, again I would like for you to tense the muscles in your
_____. Now tense and hold (pause
5–7 seconds). And, relax; letting all the tension go, focusing on these
muscles as they just relax completely. Notice what it feels like as the
muscles become more and more relaxed. Focus all your attention on the
feelings associated with relaxation flowing into these muscles.

Just enjoy the pleasant feelings of relaxation as the muscles go on
relaxing more and more deeply, more and more completely. There is

nothing for you to do but focus your attention on the very pleasant feelings of relaxation flowing into this area.

Just let go, thinking about nothing but the very pleasant feelings of relaxation. Just let those muscles go and notice how they feel now as compared to before. Notice how these muscles feel when so completely relaxed. Pay attention only to the sensations of relaxation as the relaxation process takes place. You feel calm, peaceful, relaxed.

After the PMR exercise, discuss with the patient possible targeted times in which the relaxed breathing and PMR may be useful in reducing stress that contributes to tics. Identify two situations in the next week in which the patient can practice using relaxation techniques. Have the patient and/or parents write these situations down on the Muscle Relaxation Exercise Sheet in the workbook.

Homework

✎ Instruct the patient to use the CRs for Tics 1–4 during both planned and unplanned times. Refer to the Tics, Tic Signals, and Competing Responses form. Remind parents to use social support for all tics.

✎ Have the family do planned CR practice at least 3–4 times for Tics 1–4, with special attention to the new tic, for at least 30 min each time. During the planned exercises, both the patient and the parent(s) should monitor the tic using the My Tic Sheet and Tic Monitoring Sheet for Parents in the workbook (refer to Session 1 for monitoring procedures).

✎ Have parents remind the child of the reward system to encourage compliance and boost motivation.

✎ Have parents implement the interventions on the Function-Based Interventions Form in the workbook.

✎ Have the patient practice both relaxed breathing and PMR 3 times this week, particularly before, during, or after the two stressful situations identified in session.

Chapter 10 *Session 6*

(Corresponds to chapters 4 and 5 of the workbook)

Materials Needed

- Tic Symptom Hierarchy Tracker Form
- Functional Assessment Form (FAF)
- List of sample function-based interventions from Chapter 3
- List of competing responses (CRs) from Chapter 4

Outline

- Review events of the past week and update tic hierarchy
- Review homework and reward efforts
- Conduct inconvenience review
- Review treatment procedures for prior tics
- Conduct functional assessment and present related treatment strategies for next tic on hierarchy
- Conduct HRT for next tic
- Review relaxation training techniques
- Assign homework

Working With Adults

When using the manual with adults, the following modifications are necessary in Session 6.

Materials Needed

FAF—Adult Version

In-Session Activities

When reviewing events of the past week (see following section), ask adult patients about the impact of tic symptoms on work, social, and family functioning

No behavioral reward program or age-appropriately modified reward

Weekly and Hierarchy Review

Review the events of the past week. Query the patient and parents about:

Any significant events in the patient's life

Tic symptoms and impact on school, social, and family functioning

At least one positive event or thing from patient that occurred since last session

Note any situations in which tics were increased and explore factors that may have contributed to the exacerbation

Review the Tic Symptom Hierarchy Tracker and have the patient provide SUDS ratings for the past week. Revise the list as needed, considering that old tics may resolve and new ones may appear.

Homework Review

Reward any compliance with monitoring homework. Reframe non-compliance to reduce negative feelings in the patient, problem-solve compliance difficulties, and encourage the patient to comply with homework over the coming week. At the time agreed upon in Session 1, assign points for any behavior covered in the behavioral reward program (i.e., points for attending, doing homework, and participating in the prior session).

Inconvenience Review

Review with the patient the Tic Hassles Form completed in Session 2. Use this review to attempt to sustain the patient's motivation to work on tics.

Review Function-Based Interventions and Competing Responses for Tics 1–4

Review function-based intervention and practice CRs for previous tics. Discuss any difficulties with function-based intervention protocols for Tics 1–4, and problem-solve these in session. Modify function-based intervention as needed given feedback from the past week to maximize ease of administration and compliance.

Review CR implementation for the Tics 1–4 and problem-solve these in session. Modify CR as needed given patient feedback from the past week to maximize ease of administration and compliance.

Function-Based Assessment and Interventions for Next Tic

- Remind the patient and the parents of the purposes of the function-based intervention.

- Conduct the functional assessment interview described in Chapter 3 for the next tic on the hierarchy.

- Review the functional assessment self-report data assigned at the end of Session 1.

- Use these data to work with the patient and the parents to develop function-based interventions using the five principles described in

Chapter 3. Remind the parents and the patient of the five principles of function-based interventions.

On the Function-Based Interventions Form, write down the agreed-upon interventions and work with the parents to determine a concrete plan for how these interventions will be implemented in the child's life.

Habit Reversal Training for Next Tic

Review the material in Chapter 4. Implement HRT for the next tic using the procedures outlined in this section. This tic should be the same tic as targeted in the function-based interventions from earlier in this session. As you target the tic, remember to do the following procedures.

Introduce awareness training

Define the tic

Describe antecedent sensations and behaviors

Acknowledge tics and tic signals

Select the CR

Teach the patient to do the CR

Teach the support person to praise the patient for doing HRT correctly

Teach the support person to prompt the patient to do HRT when necessary

Review of Relaxation Techniques

Review relaxed breathing and PMR techniques, and get feedback from the patient about how well he worked in the past week to reduce tension and stress.

Discuss with the patient in what specific situations relaxed breathing and PMR might help him to relax in the coming weeks. Talk about when exactly he would use these techniques.

Homework

Before assigning homework, remind parents that you will be contacting them between sessions to review progress and problem-solve difficulties with homework. You should make telephone contact with parents 1 week after Session 6 to review progress in the last week and problem-solve any difficulties with homework.

 Instruct the patient to use the CRs for Tics 1–5 during both planned and unplanned times. Refer to the Tics, Tic Signals, and Competing Responses form. Remind parents to use social support for all tics.

Have the family do planned CR practice at least 3–4 times for Tics 1–5, with special attention to the new tic, for at least 30 min each time. During the planned exercises, both the patient and the parent(s) should monitor the tic using the My Tic Sheet and Tic Monitoring Sheet for Parents in the workbook (refer to Session 1 for monitoring procedures).

Have parents remind the child of the reward system to encourage compliance and boost motivation.

Have parents implement the interventions on the Function-Based Interventions Form in the workbook.

Have the patient practice relaxed breathing and PMR 3 times this week, particularly before, during, or after the two stressful situations identified in session.

Chapter 11 | *Session 7*

(Corresponds to chapters 4–6 of the workbook)

Materials Needed

- Tic Symptom Hierarchy Tracker Form (completed in Session 1)

- Functional Assessment Form (FAF)

- List of sample function-based interventions from Chapter 3

- List of competing responses (CRs) from Chapter 4

Outline

- Review events of the past week and update tic hierarchy

- Review homework and reward efforts

- Conduct inconvenience review

- Review treatment procedures for prior tics

- Conduct functional assessment and present related treatment strategies for next tic on hierarchy

- Conduct HRT for next tic

- Review relaxation techniques

- Discuss relapse prevention strategies

- Assign homework

Working With Adults

When using the manual with adults, the following modifications are necessary in Session 7.

Materials Needed

FAF—Adult Version

In-Session Activities

When reviewing events of the past week (see following section), ask adult patients about the impact of tic symptoms on work, social, and family functioning

No behavioral reward program or age-appropriately modified reward

Weekly and Hierarchy Review

Review the events of the past week. Query the patient and parents about:

Any significant events in the patient's life

Tic symptoms and impact on school, social, and family functioning

At least one positive event or thing from patient that occurred since last session

Note any situations in which tics were increased and explore factors that may have contributed to the exacerbation

Review the Tic Symptom Hierarchy Tracker and have the patient provide SUDS ratings for the past week. Revise the list as needed, considering that old tics may resolve and new ones may appear.

Homework Review

Reward any compliance with monitoring homework. Reframe noncompliance to reduce negative feelings in the patient, problem-solve compliance difficulties, and encourage the patient to comply with homework over the coming week. At the time agreed upon in Session 1, assign points for any behavior covered in the behavioral reward program (i.e., points for attendance, doing homework, and participating in the prior session).

Inconvenience Review

Review with the patient the Tic Hassles Form completed in Session 2. Use this review to attempt to sustain the patient's motivation to work on tics.

Review Function-Based Interventions and Competing Responses for Tics 1–5

Review function-based intervention and practice CRs for previous tics. Discuss any difficulties with function-based intervention protocols for Tics 1–5, and problem-solve these in session. Modify function-based intervention as needed given feedback from the past week to maximize ease of administration and compliance.

Review CR implementation for the Tics 1–5 and problem-solve these in session. Modify CR as needed given patient feedback from the past week to maximize ease of administration and compliance.

Function-Based Assessment and Interventions for Next Tic

- Remind the patient and the parents of the purposes of the function-based intervention.

- Conduct the functional assessment interview described in Chapter 3 for the next tic on the hierarchy.

- Review the functional assessment self-report data assigned at the end of Session 1.

Use these data to work with the patient and the parents to develop function-based interventions using the five principles described in Chapter 3. Remind the parents and the patient of the five principles of function-based interventions.

On the Function-Based Interventions Form, write down the agreed-upon interventions and work with the parents to determine a concrete plan for how these interventions will be implemented in the child's life.

Habit Reversal Training for Next Tic

Review the material in Chapter 4. Implement HRT for the next tic using the procedures outlined in this section. This tic should be the same tic as targeted in the function-based interventions from earlier in this session. As you target the tic, remember to do the following procedures.

Introduce awareness training

Define the tic

Describe antecedent sensations and behaviors

Acknowledge tics and tic signals

Select the CR

Teach the patient to do the CR

Teach the support person to praise the patient for doing HRT correctly

Teach the support person to prompt the patient to do HRT when necessary

Review of Relaxation Techniques

Review relaxed breathing and PMR techniques, and get feedback from the patient about how well she worked in the past week to reduce tension and stress.

Discuss with the patient in what specific situations relaxed breathing and PMR might help her to relax in the coming weeks. Talk about when exactly she would use these techniques. Also discuss other things the patient may do in order to better relax in a stressful situation (e.g., going to her room, reading, or playing with a pet).

Relapse Prevention I: Strategies for Monitoring and Developing CR for New Tics

Discuss the topic of relapse prevention with the family in session.

Review that, by definition, the child's condition is chronic, that symptoms may return or become exacerbated during times of greater stress, and that the child's tic repertoire may change frequently over time, as specific tics wax and wane.

Emphasize the following ideas:

1. Parents should be vigilant for tic reappearance or exacerbation during stressful periods.

2. Patient need not be overprotected from stress.

3. Family should support and encourage the patient to engage in stress management techniques that patient finds personally effective.

4. Family should be aware of triggers (situational, emotional, and physical) that could lead to symptom exacerbation.

Homework

Before assigning homework, remind parents that you will be contacting them between sessions to review progress and problem-solve difficulties with homework. You should make telephone contact with parents 1 week after Session 7 to review progress in the last week and problem-solve any difficulties with homework.

 ✎ Instruct the patient to use the CRs for Tics 1–6 during both planned and unplanned times. Refer to the Tics, Tic Signals, and Competing Responses form. Remind parents to use social support for all tics.

✎ Have the family do planned CR practice at least 3–4 times for Tics 1–6, with special attention to the new tic, for at least 30 min each time. During the planned exercises, both the patient and the parent(s) should monitor the tic using the My Tic Sheet and Tic Monitoring Sheet for Parents in the workbook (refer to Session 1 for monitoring procedures).

✎ Have parents remind the child of the reward system to encourage compliance and boost motivation.

✎ Have parents implement the interventions on the Function-Based Interventions Form in the workbook.

✎ Have the patient practice both relaxed breathing and PMR 3 times this week, particularly before, during, or after stressful situations identified in session. Use PMR Exercise Sheet in the workbook as a reminder.

Chapter 12 *Session 8*

(Corresponds to chapters 4–6 of the workbook)

Materials Needed

- Tic Symptom Hierarchy Tracker Form
- Functional Assessment Form (FAF)
- List of sample function-based interventions from Chapter 3
- List of competing responses (CRs) from Chapter 4

Outline

- Review events of the past week and update tic hierarchy
- Review homework and reward efforts
- Conduct inconvenience review
- Review treatment procedures for prior tics
- Conduct functional assessment and present related treatment strategies for remaining tics on hierarchy
- Conduct HRT for remaining tics
- Review relaxation techniques
- Discuss relapse prevention strategies
- Assign homework

Working With Adults

When using the manual with adults, the following modifications are necessary in Session 8.

Materials Needed

FAF—Adult Version

In-Session Activities

When reviewing events of the past week (see following section), ask adult patients about the impact of tic symptoms on work, social, and family functioning

No behavioral reward program or age-appropriately modified reward

Weekly Review

Review the events of the past week. Query the patient and parents about:

Any significant events in the patient's life

Tic symptoms and impact on school, social, and family functioning

At least one positive event or thing from patient that occurred since last session

Note any situations in which tics were increased and explore factors that may have contributed to the exacerbation

Review the Tic Symptom Hierarchy Tracker and have the patient provide SUDS ratings for the past week. Revise the list as needed, considering that old tics may resolve and new ones may appear.

Homework Review

Reward any compliance with monitoring homework. Reframe noncompliance to reduce negative feelings in the patient, problem-solve compliance difficulties, and encourage the patient to comply with homework over the coming week. At the time agreed upon in Session 1, assign points for any behavior covered in the behavioral reward program (i.e., points for attendance, doing homework, and participating in the prior session). Usually, it is at this session that points are exchanged for a reward.

Final Inconvenience Review

Review with the patient the Tic Hassles Form completed in Session 2. Reinforce how treatment efforts have reduced the negative consequences originally associated with the patient's tic behaviors at the start of the program.

Review Function-Based Interventions and Competing Responses for Tics 1–6

Discuss any difficulties with function-based intervention, and problem-solve these in session. Modify function-based intervention as needed given feedback from past week to maximize ease of administration and compliance.

Review CRs for previous tics and have the patient practice implementing them (in vivo or imaginal). Discuss any difficulties with CRs, and problem-solve these in session. Modify CRs as needed given patient feedback from past week to maximize ease of administration and compliance.

Function-Based Assessment and Interventions for Remaining Tics

- Remind the patient and the parents of the purposes of the function-based intervention.

- Conduct the functional assessment interview described in Chapter 3 for remaining tics on the hierarchy.

Review the functional assessment self-report data assigned at the end of Session 1.

Use these data to work with the patient and the parents to develop function-based interventions using the five principles described in Chapter 3. Remind the parents and the patient of the five principles of function-based interventions.

On the Function-Based Interventions Form, write down the agreed-upon interventions and work with the parents to understand how these interventions may be implemented in the child's life.

Review the rules involved in developing function-based interventions.

Habit Reversal Training for Remaining Tics

Review the material in Chapter 4. Implement HRT for the remaining tics using the procedures outlined in this section. These tics should be the same as targeted in the function-based interventions from earlier in this session. As you target the tics, remember to do the following procedures.

Introduce awareness training

Define the tic

Describe antecedent sensations and behaviors

Acknowledge tics and tic signals

Select the CR

Teach the patient to do the CR

Teach the support person to praise the patient for doing HRT correctly

Teach the support person to prompt the patient to do HRT when necessary

Discuss with the patient how he would go about developing CRs to new tics that may appear in the future. Give examples of tics to the patient that he does not have now, and ask him to come up with a CR that he can do easily. Review with the patient the characteristics of a good CR, and when he should initiate the CR (as soon as he gets the urge to tic, but even during or after tic occurrence).

Review of Relaxation Techniques

Briefly review relaxed breathing and PMR techniques, as well as other methods idiosyncratic to the patient that aid in his relaxation.

Discuss with the patient in what future situations relaxation techniques might help to decrease his stress levels. Emphasize that he can perform techniques before, during, or after stressful situations to better relax.

Relapse Prevention II: Strategies for Monitoring and Developing CRs for New Tics

Discuss the topic of relapse prevention with the family in session. Review with parents the relapse prevention topics addressed in the last session. Discuss how, if tic symptoms reappear or worsen, the parents should work with the patient to:

1. Ascertain whether or not the patient is aware of tic exacerbation or appearance.

2. Work with the patient to initially monitor symptoms at planned times and unplanned times.

3. Work with the patient to develop competing responses to perform in response to tics (refer to list of sample competing responses in Chapter 4).

4. Provide family support and reinforcement to the patient for implementing CRs to tics.

5. Consider referral for a return to treatment for assistance with more complicated symptoms.

Therapy Termination

Summarize the patient's progress during therapy. Elicit family and patient feelings regarding treatment and termination.

Graduation

Present a certificate for younger patients. Provide other age-appropriate acknowledgement for older patients and adolescents.

Chapter 13   *Booster Sessions*

(Corresponds to chapters 4–6 of the workbook)

Therapist Note

■ *Monthly booster sessions are recommended for the first 3 months after treatment ends.* ■

Materials Needed

- Tic Symptom Hierarchy Tracker Form

- Functional Assessment Form (FAF)

- List of sample function-based interventions from Chapter 3

- List of competing responses (CRs) from Chapter 4

Outline

- Review events of the past month and update tic hierarchy

- Review homework and reward efforts

- Conduct inconvenience review

- Review overall treatment techniques for all treated tics

- Review relaxation techniques

- Review relapse prevention strategies

Working With Adults

When using the manual with adults, the following modifications are necessary in Sessions 9–11.

Materials Needed

FAF—Adult Version

In-Session Activities

When reviewing events of the past month (see following section), ask adult patients about the impact of tic symptoms on work, social, and family functioning

Monthly and Hierarchy Review

Review events of the past month, including:

Any significant events in the patient's life

Tic symptoms and impact on school, social, and family functioning

At least one positive event or thing from patient that occurred since last session

Note any situations in which tics were increased and explore factors that may have contributed to the exacerbation

Review the Tic Symptom Hierarchy Tracker and have the patient provide SUDS ratings for the past month. Revise the list as needed, considering that old tics may resolve and new ones appear.

Inconvenience Review

Review with the patient the Tic Hassles Form completed in Session 2. Reinforce how treatment efforts have reduced the negative consequences originally associated with the patient's tic behaviors at the start of the program.

Function-Based Intervention and Competing Response Review

Review and troubleshoot function-based interventions for all tics on the hierarchy. Discuss any remaining difficulties and problem-solve these in session. Modify interventions as needed to maximize ease of administration and compliance.

Discuss with the patient how new tics have been addressed and help develop function-based strategies for any new tics that may have appeared since the last session if they differ from those strategies specifically being used to target motor and vocal tics globally.

Next, review CRs for all tics on the hierarchy and have the patient practice implementing them. Discuss any remaining difficulties and problem-solve these in session. Modify CRs as needed to maximize ease of administration and compliance.

Discuss with patient the use of competing responses for any new tics that may have appeared since the last session and help patient develop CRs as needed.

Review of Relaxation Techniques

Briefly review deep breathing and PMR techniques, as well as other methods idiosyncratic to the patient that aid in her relaxation.

Discuss with patient in what future situations relaxation techniques might help to decrease her stress levels. Emphasize that she can perform techniques before, during, or after stressful situations to better relax.

Relapse Prevention Review

Review with parents relapse prevention topics addressed in Sessions 7 and 8. Discuss any difficulties with relapse prevention strategies and problem-solve these in session.

Appendix of Resources

Books

Handler, L. (1998). *Twitch and shout: A Touretter's tale.* New York: Dutton.

Hughes, S. (1996). *What makes Ryan tick?* Duarte, CA: Hope Press.

Kushner, H. I. (1999). *A cursing brain?: The histories of Tourette syndrome.* Cambridge, MA: Harvard University Press.

Marsh, T. L. (2007). *Children with Tourette syndrome: A parents guide.* Bethesda, MD: Woodbine House.

Shimberg, E. F. (1995). *Living with Tourette syndrome.* New York: Fireside.

Websites

National Tourette Syndrome Association

www.tsa-usa.org

Tourette Syndrome Plus

www.tourettesyndrome.net

Videos (all videos listed and more are available on the TSA website)

After the Diagnosis . . . The Next Steps For those with a new diagnosis of TS, clarifies what TS is, offers encouragement, and dispels misperceptions. Excerpts from the "Family Life With TS" video, experiences with TS, comments from medical experts, 35 min.

Family Life With Tourette Syndrome . . . Personal Stories . . . A Six-Part Series Adults, teenagers, children and their families . . . all affected by Tourette syndrome describe lives filled with triumphs and setbacks . . . struggle and growth. Informative and inspirational. Each vignette also available separately—AV11a–AV11f, 58 min.

Using Behavior Therapy to Manage Tic Disorders in Children A presentation by Dr. Doug Woods about using behavior therapy to manage tics in children, CD-ROM format.

Diagnosing and Treating Tourette Syndrome A series of medical education programs for physicians and allied health care professionals along with a series of important medical articles, 2-Disc Set.

References

Achenbach, T. M. (1991). *Manual for the child behavior checklist/4–18 and 1991 profile*. Burlington, VT: University of Vermont Press.

American Psychiatric Association. (2000). *Diagnostic and statistical manual of mental disorders* (4th ed.-Text Revision). Washington, DC: Author.

Azrin, N. H., & Nunn, R. G. (1973). Habit reversal: A method of eliminating nervous habits and tics. *Behaviour Research and Therapy, 11,* 619–628.

Azrin, N. H., Nunn, R. G., & Frantz, S. E. (1980). Habit reversal vs. negative practice treatment of nervous tics. *Behavior Therapy, 11,* 169–178.

Azrin, N. H., & Peterson, A. L. (1988). Habit reversal for the treatment of Tourette syndrome. *Behaviour Research and Therapy, 26,* 347–351.

Azrin, N. H., & Peterson, A. L. (1989). Reduction of an eye tic by controlled blinking. *Behavior Therapy, 20,* 467–473.

Azrin, N. H., & Peterson, A. L. (1990). Treatment of Tourette syndrome by habit reversal: A wait-list control group comparison. *Behavior Therapy, 21,* 305–318.

Beck, A. T., & Steer, R. A. (1987). *Beck depression inventory manual.* San Antonio, TX: The Psychological Corporation.

Beck, A. T., & Steer, R. A. (1993). *Manual for the revised Beck Anxiety Inventory.* San Antonio, TX: Psychological Corporation.

Blais, M. A., Lenderking, W. R., Baer, L., deLorell, A., Peets, K., Leahy, L., et al. (1999). Development and initial validation of a brief mental health outcome measure. *Journal of Personality Assessment, 73,* 359–373.

Bliss, J. (1980). Sensory experiences in Gilles de la Tourette syndrome. *Archives of General Psychiatry, 37,* 1343–1347.

Bloch, M. H., Peterson, B. S., Scahill, L., Otka, J., Katsovich, L., Zhang, H., et al. (2006). Adulthood outcome of tic and obsessive-compulsive symptom severity in children with Tourette syndrome. *Archives of Pediatrics and Adolescent Medicine, 160,* 54–69.

Boudjouk, P., Woods, D. W., Miltenberger, R. G., & Long, E. S. (2000). Negative peer evaluation in adolescents: Effects of tic disorders and trichotillomania. *Child and Family Behavior Therapy, 22,* 17–28.

Bruggeman, R., van der Linden, C., Buitelaar, J., Gericke, G., Hawkridge, S., & Temlett, J. (2001). Risperidone versus pimozide in Tourette's disorder: A comparative double-blind parallel-group study. *Journal of Clinical Psychiatry, 62*(1), 50–56.

Bruun, R. D. (1988). Subtle and under recognized side effects of neuroleptic treatment in children with Tourette disorder. *American Journal of Psychiatry, 145,* 3–74.

Burd, L., Kauffman, D. W., & Kerbeshian, J. (1992). Tourette syndrome and learning disabilities. *Journal of Learning Disabilities, 25,* 598–604.

Burd, L., & Kerbeshian, J. (1987). Onset of Gilles de la Tourette's syndrome before 1 year of age. *American Journal of Psychiatry, 144*(8), 1066–1067.

Carr, J., Bailey, J., Carr, C., & Coggin, A. (1996). The role of independent variable integrity in the behavioral management of Tourette syndrome. *Behavioral Interventions, 11*(1), 35–45.

Champion, L. M., Fulton, W. A., & Shady, G. A. (1988). Tourette syndrome and social functioning in a Canadian population. *Neuroscience and Biobehavioral Reviews, 12,* 255–257.

Chang, S., & Piacentini, J. (2008) *Habit reversal versus awareness training for childhood tic disorders.* in preparation.

Chang, S., Himle, M. B., Tucker, B. T. P., Woods, D. W., & Piacentini, J. C. (2008). *Initial development and psychometric properties of the Parent Tic Questionnaire (PTQ) to assess tic severity in children with chronic tic disorders.* Manuscript submitted for publication.

Cloutier, J. (1985). Elimination of a nervous tic through habit reversal. *Technologie et Therapie du Comportement, 8,* 153–159.

Conners, C. K., Erhardt, D., & Sparrow, E. (1999). *Conners' Adult ADHD Rating Scales (CAARS).* North Tonawanda, NY: Multi-Health Systems Inc.

Costello, E. J., Angold, A., Burns, B. J., Stangl, D. K., Tweed, D. L., Erkanli, A., et al. (1996). The great smoky mountains study of youth: Goals, design, methods, and the prevalence of DSM-III-R disorders. *Archives of General Psychiatry, 53,* 1129–1136.

Deckersbach, T., Rauch, S., Buhlmann, U., & Wilhelm, S. (2006) Habit reversal versus supportive psychotherapy in Tourette's disorder: A randomized controlled trial and predictors of treatment response. *Behaviour Research and Therapy, 44,* 1079–1090.

Dedmon, R. (1990). Tourette syndrome in children: Knowledge and services. *Health & Social Work, 15*(2), 107–115.

Dion, Y., Annable, L., Sandor, P., & Chouinard, G. (2002). Risperidone in the treatment of Tourette syndrome: A double-blind placebo-controlled trial. *Journal of Clinical Psychopharmacology, 22*(1), 31–39.

DuPaul, G. J., Power, T. J., Anastopoulos, A. D., & Reid, R. (1998). *ADHD Rating Scale-IV.* New York: Guiford Press.

Elstner, K., Selai, C., Trimble, M., & Robertson, M. (2001). Quality of life (QOL) of patients with Gilles de la Tourette's syndrome. *Acta Psychiatrica Scandinavica, 103*(1), 52–59.

Finney, J. W., Rapoff, M. A., Hall, C. L., & Christopherson, E. R. (1983). Replication and social validation of habit reversal treatment for tics. *Behavior Therapy, 14,* 116–126.

Friedrich, S., Morgan, S. B., & Devine, C. (1996). Children's attitudes and behavioral intentions toward a peer with Tourette syndrome. *Journal of Pediatric Psychology, 21,* 307–319.

Goodman, W. K., Price, L. H., Rasmussen, S. A., Mazure, C., Fleischmann, R. L., Hill, C. L., et al. (1989a). The yale-brown obsessive compulsive scale. I. Development, use, and reliability. *Archive of General Psychiatry, 46,* 1006–1011.

Goodman, W. K., Price, L. H., Rasmussen, S. A., Mazure, C., Fleischmann, R. L., Hill, C. L., et al. (1989b). The yale-brown obsessive compulsive scale. II. Validity. *Archives of General Psychiatry, 46*(11), 1012–1016.

Himle, M. B., & Woods, D. W. (2005). An experimental evaluation of tic suppression and the tic rebound effect. *Behaviour Research and Therapy, 43,* 1443–1451.

Himle, M. B., Woods, D. W., Conelea, C. A., Bauer, C. C., & Rice, K. A. (2007). Investigating the effects of tic suppression on premonitory urge ratings in children and adolescents with Tourette's syndrome. *Behaviour Research and Therapy, 45* (12), 2964–2976.

Himle, M. B., Woods, D. W., Piacentini, J. C., & Walkup, J. (2006). Brief review of habit reversal training for Tourette's syndrome. *Journal of Child Neurology, 21,* 719–725.

Hornse, H., Banerjee, S., Zeitlin, H., & Robertson, M. (2001). The prevalence of Tourette syndrome in 13–14 year olds in mainstream schools. *Journal of Child Psychology and Psychiatry, 42*(8), 1035–1039.

Hughes, R. (1996). *What makes Ryan tick? A family's triumph over Tourette syndrome and attention deficit-hyperactivity disorder.* Duarte, CA: Hope Press.

King, R. A., Scahill, L., Lombroso, P. J., & Leckman, J. (2003). Tourette syndrome and other tic disorders. In A. Martin, L. Scahill, D. Charney, & J. F. Leckman (Eds.), *Pediatric psychopharmacology: Principles and practice* (pp. 526–542). New York: Oxford University Press.

Koch, C. R., & Blacher, J. (2007). Evidence-based psychosocial treatments for tic disorders. *Clinical Psychology: Science and Practice, 4*(3), 252–267.

Kovacs, M. (1992). *Children's depression inventory.* North Tonawanda, NY: Multi-Health Systems Inc.

Leckman, J. F., & Cohen, D. J (Eds.). (1999a). Evolving models of pathogenesis. *Tourette's syndrome-tics, obsessions, compulsions: Developmental psychopathology and clinical care* (pp. 155–176). Hoboken, NJ: John Wiley & Sons Inc.

Leckman, J. F., & Cohen, D. J. (Eds.). (1999b). *Tourette's syndrome-tics, obsessions, compulsions: Developmental psychopathology and clinical care.* Hoboken, NJ: John Wiley & Sons Inc.

Leckman, J. F., King, R. A., & Cohen, D. J. (1999). Tics and tic disorders. In J. F. Leckman, & D. J. Cohen (Eds.), *Tourette's syndrome-tics, obsessions, compulsions: Developmental psychopathology and clinical care* (pp. 23–42). New York, NY: John Wiley & Sons Inc.

Leckman, J. F., Riddle, M. A., Hardin, M. T., Ort, S. I., Swartz, K. L., Stevenson, J., et al. (1989). The Yale Global Tic Severity Scale (YGTSS): Initial testing of a clinical-rated scale of tic severity. *Journal of the American Academy of Child and Adolescent Psychiatry, 28,* 566–573.

Leckman, J. F., Walker, D. E., & Cohen, D. J. (1993). Premonitory urges in Tourette's syndrome. *American Journal of Psychiatry, 150,* 98–102.

Leckman, J. F., Zhang, H., Vitale, A., Lahnin, F., Lynch, K., Bondi, C., et al. (1998). Course of tic severity in Tourette syndrome: The first two decades. *Pediatrics, 102,* 14–19.

Leon, A. C., Shear, M. K., Portera, L., & Klerman, G. L. (1992). Assessing impairment in patients with panic disorder: The Sheehan disability scale. *Social Psychiatry and Psychiatric Epidemiology, 27,* 78–82.

Lin, H., Katsovich, L., Ghebremichael, M., Findley, D. B., Grantz, H., Lombroso, P. J., et al. (2007). Psychosocial stress predicts future symptom severities in children and adolescents with Tourette syndrome and/or obsessive-compulsive disorder. *Journal of Child Psychology and Psychiatry, 48,* 157–166.

March, J., Parker, J., Sullivan, K., Stallings, P., & Conners, C. K. (1997). The Multidimensional Anxiety Scale for Children (MASC): Factor structure, reliability, and validity. *Journal of the American Academy of Child & Adolescent Psychiatry, 36*(4), 554–565.

Marcks, B. A., Woods, D. W., Teng, E. J., & Twohig, M. P. (2004). What do those who know, know? Investigating providers' knowledge about Tourette's syndrome and it's treatment. *Cognitive and Behavioral Practice, 11*(3), 298–305.

Miltenberger, R. G., & Fuqua, R. W. (1985, September). A comparison of contingent vs. non-contingent competing response practice in the treatment of nervous habits. *Journal of Behavior Therapy and Experimental Psychiatry, 16*(3), 195–200.

Miltenberger, R. G., Fuqua, R. W., & McKinley, T. (1985). Habit reversal with muscle tics: Replication and component analysis. *Behavior Therapy, 16*, 39–50.

O'Connor, K. P., Brault, M., Robillard, S., Loiselle, J., Borgeat, F., & Stip, E. (2001). Evaluation of a cognitive-behavioral program for the management of chronic tic and habit disorders. *Behaviour Research and Therapy, 39*, 667–681.

Peterson, A. L., & Azrin, N. H. (1992). An evaluation of behavioral treatments for Tourette syndrome. *Behaviour Research and Therapy, 30*, 167–174.

Sallee, F. R., Nesbitt, L., Jackson, C., Sine, L., & Sethuraman, G. (1997). Relative efficacy of haloperidol and pimozide in children and adolescents with Tourette's disorder. *American Journal of Psychiatry, 154*(8), 1057–1062.

Scahill, L., Chappell, P. B., Kim, Y. S., Shultz, R. T., Katsovich, L., Shepherd, E., et al. (2001). A placebo-controlled study of guanfacine in the treatment of children with tic disorders and attention deficit hyperactivity disorder. *American Journal of Psychiatry, 158*, 1067–1074.

Scahill, L., Erenberg, G., & The Tourette Syndrome Practice Parameter Work Group. (2006). Contemporary assessment and pharmacotherapy of Tourette syndrome. *NeuroRx, 3*(2), 192–206.

Scahill, L., Leckman, J., & Marek, K. (1995). Sensory phenomena in Tourette's syndrome. *Advances in Neurology, 65*, 273–280.

Scahill, L., Riddle, M. A., McSwiggin-Hardin, M., Goodman, W. K., Ort, S. I., King, R. A., et al. (1997). Children's yale-brown obsessive compulsive scale: Reliability and validity. *Journal of the American Academy of Child and Adolescent Psychiatry, 36*(6), 844–852.

Scahill, L., Sukhodolsky, D., Williams, S., & Leckman, J. F. (2005). The public health importance of tics and tic disorders. *Advances in Neurology, 96*, 240–248.

Shady, G., Broder, R., Staley, D., & Furer, P. (1995, July). Tourette syndrome and employment: Descriptors, predictors, and problems. *Psychiatric Rehabilitation Journal, 19*(1), 35–42.

Shapiro, E., Shapiro, A. K., Fulop, G., Hubbard, M., Mandeli, J., Nordlie, J., et al. (1989). Controlled study of haloperidol, pimozide and placebo for the treatment of Gilles de la Tourette's syndrome. *Archives of General Psychiatry, 46*(8), 722–730.

Shimberg, E. (1995). *Living with Tourette syndrome.* New York: Fireside Books.

Stokes, A., Bawden, H. N., Camfield, P. R., Backman, J. E., & Dooley, J. M. (1991). Peer problems in Tourette's disorder. *Pediatrics, 87,* 936–941.

Sukhodolsky, D. G., Scahill, L., Zhang, H., Peterson, B. S., King, R. A., Lombrosos, P. J., et al. (2003). Disruptive behavior in children with Tourette's syndrome: Association with ADHD comorbidity, tic severity, and functional impairment. *Journal of the American Academy of Child and Adolescent Psychiatry, 42,* 98–105.

Wilhelm, S., Deckersbach, T., Coffey, B. J., Bohne, A., Peterson, A. L., & Baer, L. (2003). Habit reversal versus supportive psychotherapy for Tourette's disorder: A randomized controlled trial. *American Journal of Psychiatry, 160,* 1175–1177.

Woods, D. W., Fuqua, R. W., & Outman, R. C. (1999). Evaluating the social acceptability of individuals with habit disorders: The effects of frequency, topography and gender manipulation. *Journal of Psychopathology and Behavioral Assessment, 21,* 1–18.

Woods, D. W., & Himle, M. B. (2004). Creating tic suppression: Comparing the effects of verbal instruction to differential reinforcement. *Journal of Applied Behavior Analysis, 37,* 417–420

Woods, D. W., Himle, M. B., Miltenberger, R. G., Carr, J. E., Osmon, D. C., Karsten, A. M., et al. (2008). Durability, negative impact, and neuropsychological predictors of tic suppression in children with chronic tic disorders. *Journal of Abnormal Child Psychology, 36,* 237–245.

Woods, D. W., Miltenberger, R. G., & Lumley, V. A. (1996). Sequential application of major habit reversal components to treat motor tics in children. *Journal of Applied Behavior Analysis, 29,* 483–493.

Woods, D. W., Piacentini, J. C., & Himle, M. B. (2007). Assessment of tic disorders. In D. W. Woods, J. Piacentini, & J. Walkup (Eds.), *Treating Tourette syndrome and tic disorders: A guide for practitioners* (pp. 22–37). New York: Guilford Publications Inc.

Woods, D. W., Piacentini, J. C., Himle, M. B., & Chang, S. (2005). Premonitory Urge for Tics Scale (PUTS): Initial psychometric results and examination of the premonitory urge phenomenon in children with tic disorders. *Journal of Developmental and Behavioral Pediatrics, 26,* 397–403.

Woods, D. W., Piacentini, J. C., & Walkup, J. (2007). *Treating Tourette syndrome and tic disorders: A guide for practitioners.* New York: The Guilford Press.

Woods, D. W., & Twohig, M. P. (2002). Using habit reversal to treat chronic vocal tic disorder in children. *Behavioral Interventions, 17,* 159–168.

Woods, D. W., Twohig, M. P., Flessner, C. A., & Roloff, T. E. (2003). Treatment of vocal tics in children with Tourette syndrome: Investigating the efficacy of habit reversal. *Journal of Applied Behavior Analysis, 36,* 109–112.

About the Authors

Douglas W. Woods received his PhD in Clinical Psychology from Western Michigan University in 1999. He is currently Associate Professor of Psychology and Director of Clinical Training at the University of Wisconsin–Milwaukee. Dr. Woods is a recognized expert in the assessment and treatment of trichotillomania, Tourette syndrome and other obsessive-compulsive spectrum disorders. Dr. Woods is a member of the Trichotillomania Learning Center's Scientific Advisory Board and a member of the Tourette Syndrome Association's Medical Advisory Board. He has published more than 100 journal articles and book chapters on these and related topics, including two books *Tic Disorders, Trichotillomania, and Other Repetitive Behavior Disorders: A Behavioral Approach to Analysis and Treatment*, and *Treating Tourette Syndrome and Tic Disorders: A Guide for Practitioners*. Dr. Woods' research has been funded by grants from the National Institutes of Health, the Trichotillomania Learning Center, and the Tourette Syndrome Association.

John C. Piacentini, PhD, ABPP, is Professor of Psychiatry and Biobehavioral Sciences, Director of the Child OCD, Anxiety, and Tic Disorders Program, and Chief of Child Psychology in the Division of Child and Adolescent Psychiatry at the UCLA Semel Institute for Neuroscience and Human Behavior. He received his PhD in Clinical Psychology from the University of Georgia and completed postdoctoral training at the New York State Psychiatric Institute/Columbia University, where he spent the next 7 years as a faculty member in the Division of Child and Adolescent Psychiatry. Dr. Piacentini is an active CBT teacher and supervisor and has conducted numerous workshops on the treatment of tic disorder, OCD, and child anxiety in the United States and around the world. He has published extensively on these disorders, including the Programs *That Work*™ therapist guide entitled *Cognitive-behavioral Treatment of Childhood OCD* and has received several grants from NIH and other groups to study the treatment of child and adolescent tic disorders, OCD, and anxiety. Dr. Piacentini is Chair of the Behavioral Sciences Consortium of the Tourette Syndrome Association, a member of the American Board of Clinical Child and Adolescent Psychology and the Trichotillomania Learning Center Scientific Advisory Board, and a Founding Fellow of the Academy of Cognitive Therapy.

Susanna W. Chang, PhD, is Assistant Professor of Psychiatry and Biobehavioral Sciences in the David Geffen School of Medicine at the University of California at Los Angeles and part of the UCLA Child OCD, Anxiety, and Tic Disorders Program in the Semel Institute for Neuroscience and Human Behavior. She received her PhD in Clinical Psychology from the University of New Mexico and completed postdoctoral research training at UCLA Division of Child & Adolescent Psychiatry with a focus on neurocognitive aspects of child psychiatric disorders. She has been involved in numerous federally funded research grants, investigating the assessment and treatment of tic, OCD, and related disorders. She is currently the principal investigator of a NIMH grant, examining the neurocognitive correlates of behavior treatment response in childhood TS.

Thilo Deckersbach, PhD, received his PhD in Clinical Psychology from the Philipps-University Marburg, Germany, in 2000. He is currently Assistant Professor of Psychology at Harvard Medical School and the Director of Cognitive Neuroscience Research in the Bipolar Clinic and Research Program at the Massachusetts General Hospital in Boston. Dr. Deckersbach is a recognized expert in the assessment and treatment of obsessive-compulsive spectrums and mood disorders. He has authored and coauthored over 50 journal articles and book chapters. His research has been funded by the Obsessive-Compulsive Foundation, Tourette Syndrome Association, National Alliance of Research in Schizophrenia and Depression, and the National Institutes of Mental Health.

Golda S. Ginsburg received her PhD in Psychology from the University of Vermont in 1990. She is currently Associate Professor of Psychiatry and Director of Research in the Division of Child and Adolescent Psychiatry at the Johns Hopkins University School of Medicine. Dr. Ginsburg is an expert in the assessment, prevention, and treatment of childhood anxiety disorders and has published numerous articles and book chapters on this and related topics in child psychiatry. Dr. Ginsburg's research has been funded by grants from the National Institutes of Health and the Obsessive-Compulsive Foundation. She is one of the key investigators on numerous large-scale studies investigating the efficacy of cognitive-behavioral therapy for several childhood disorders, including anxiety, depression, and Tourette syndrome.

Alan L. Peterson, PhD, is currently a professor at the Behavioral Wellness Center for Clinical Trials in the Department of Psychology at the University of Texas Health Science Center at San Antonio. In collaboration with Dr. Nathan Azrin, Dr. Peterson conducted several of the initial studies to develop and evaluate the treatment protocol for the use of habit reversal for the treatment of Tourette syndrome. He has more than 100 scientific publications to his credit. Dr. Peterson's research has been funded by grants from the National Institutes of Health, the Department of Defense, and the Tourette Syndrome Association.

Lawrence D. Scahill, PhD, is Professor of Nursing and Child Psychiatry at Yale University, where he is the Director of the Research Unit on Pediatric Psychopharmacology (RUPP) at the Child Study Center. The Yale RUPP is part of a multisite consortium focused on developing and testing new treatments for children with autism and related disorders. Dr. Scahill is also actively involved in treatment research in Tourette syndrome as part of the Behavioral Sciences Consortium and the Clinical Trials Consortium. Dr. Scahill received his master's degree in psychiatric nursing and doctorate in epidemiology at Yale University. He joined the faculty of the Child Study Center in 1989, was appointed Assistant Professor in 1997, Associate Professor in 2000, and Professor in 2006. Dr. Scahill serves on the Medical Advisory Board of the Tourette Syndrome Association, is on the editorial board of several journals, and is the author of over 150 articles on autism, Tourette syndrome, ADHD, and obsessive-compulsive disorder.

John T. Walkup, MD, is an Associate Professor of Psychiatry and Behavioral Sciences, Division of Child and Adolescent Psychiatry, Johns Hopkins Medical Institutions in Baltimore, Maryland. He currently serves as the Deputy Director of the Division of Child and Adolescent Psychiatry and the Principal Investigator of the National Institute of Mental Health–funded Johns Hopkins Research Unit of Pediatric Psychopharmacology and Psychosocial Interventions. He was the Johns Hopkins site Principal Investigator on the Treatment of Adolescents with Depression Study (TADS), Child/Adolescent Anxiety Multimodal Study (CAMS); the Comprehensive Behavioral Intervention for Tics Study (CBITS); and Treatment of Early Age Mania study (TEAM). He also has two large projects working with American Indian tribes in the Southwest United States. Cradling our Future is a NIDA-funded clinical trial of an in-home intervention delivered by native paraprofessionals to pregnant teens and the second is Empowering our Spirit, a SAMHSA-funded Suicide Prevention Study funded under the Garrett Lee Smith Memorial Act. He is the current Chair of the Medical Advisory Board of the U.S. Tourette Syndrome Association. Dr. Walkup is the author of a number of articles and book chapters on psychopharmacology, Tourette yndrome, obsessive-compulsive disorder, and other anxiety disorders.

Sabine Wilhelm, PhD, is Associate Professor of Psychology (Psychiatry) at the Harvard Medical School. She is also Director of the Obsessive-Compulsive and Related Disorders Clinic and Director of the Cognitive-Behavior Therapy Program at the Massachusetts General Hospital and Harvard Medical School. Dr. Wilhelm is recognized as a leading researcher in Tourette/ syndrome, OCD, and body dysmorphic disorder (BDD) and has published extensively on the clinical characteristics and treatment of these disorders. Currently, Dr. Wilhelm is the principal investigator of several NIMH-funded clinical research studies. In addition to this book, Dr. Wilhelm coauthored a treatment manual for OCD entitled *Cognitive Therapy for Obsessive-Compulsive Disorder: A Guide for Professionals*, and she also recently wrote the self-help book *Feeling Good About the Way You Look: A Program for Overcoming Body Image Problems*. Dr. Wilhelm serves on several editorial and advisory boards, as well as the Scientific Advisory Board of the Obsessive-Compulsive Foundation, the International Obsessive-Compulsive Cognitions Working Group (OCCWG), and the Tourette Syndrome Association Behavioral Science Consortium. Her areas of clinical and research interest include the development, maintenance, and treatment outcome of OCD, BDD, and Tourette syndrome/tic disorders.